THE PHILOSOPHIC
WAY OF LIFE

THE UNIVERSITY OF CHICAGO PRESS
.CHICAGO, ILLINOIS

—

THE BAKER & TAYLOR COMPANY
NEW YORK

THE MACMILLAN COMPANY OF CANADA, LIMITED
TORONTO

THE CAMBRIDGE UNIVERSITY PRESS
LONDON

THE MARUZEN-KABUSHIKI-KAISHA
TOKYO, OSAKA, KYOTO, FUKUOKA, SENDAI

THE COMMERCIAL PRESS, LIMITED
SHANGHAI

THE PHILOSOPHIC
WAY OF LIFE

T. V. SMITH
THE UNIVERSITY OF CHICAGO

THE UNIVERSITY OF CHICAGO
PRESS ، CHICAGO ، ILLINOIS

TO YOU
A SIXTH PHILOSOPHER
IN QUEST OF WHOM
FIVE HERE GO

PREFACE

TO THE left and in front is despair, to the right and in front is illusion, behind is the pressure men call evolution, ahead is life—ahead. Who dares to lift the veil that hangs before us, the veil of despair and illusion? Lift it or not, the march is forward. Advance in the name of science alone and be menaced by despair. Advance in the name of religion alone and be lulled by illusion. Advance cautiously in the name of philosophy and, perchance, a passageway may be opened at the rift where in front, far in front, despair and illusion meet. Knowledge is not enough for life so precariously beset; faith is not enough for life so perilously begirded; wisdom alone can suffice when knowledge and faith are not enough.

No one has a monopoly upon wisdom. The philosopher is its chief pretender in a specialized age: he has too little knowledge to be a scientist; he has too little faith to be a saint. Does he have imagination enough, sympathy enough, humor enough, clairvoyance enough to be a sage? In America we credit with a trial every pretender who asserts long enough and loudly enough that he is an expert. Let us in a moment of chance-taking give the philosopher a chance to prove that he is a specialist of things in general. He asks of us for the experiment nothing but our lives: we cannot give more, he can take no less. With him at least we can march ahead. We cannot abide here for the pressure. Shall we away with the philosopher?

Americans who elect the hazard have a liberal choice of guides from among their own recent countrymen. The four philosophic guides whom we propose here to evaluate represent not merely various points of view but also the chief historic schools, Idealism, Pragmatism, Realism. Not as schoolmen, however, do we consider them. We take them, rather, as representing points of view—each sufficiently distinct to be emphatic but wieldy enough to facilitate a composite way of life as a final result.

Josiah Royce is made to represent the religious way of life, William James the scientific way of life, John Dewey the social way of life, and George Santayana the aesthetic way of life. No one of them lacks other elements than the one thus attributed to him. There is, however, a pith and marrow about each that fits the characterization suggested. It is with an acknowledgment of oversimplification, but with a belief that thus no more injustice is done to them as our material than they have done to life as their material, that we compress each to a single point of view. They have oversimplified life: in rounding out a system each has selected and dismissed, each has praised with attention and dispraised with neglect. They have chosen, each in his own manner, what they would to illustrate the nature of the whole. With gentle and genial irony, for ends wholly our own, the same do we here unto them.

"For ends wholly our own"—that is, for the reader's own. Some books are written for the author; this book is written for you, my reader. It deals with a subject of which you have often thought—with things in general, with life. In it through the prompting of a democratic mood you will be praised for your self-reliance; you will be honored as source of all virtue; you will be flattered as final judge of every issue that really matters. Consider how much of this you can stand and still be yourself. If you err in this crucial self-knowledge, you may become through this and similar influences such a person as you now dislike, with only this consolation: that that person will dislike the person you now are. It is sometimes serious business, this business of burying yourself in a book.

But if you elect to bury yourself in this book for an hour, you join good company. A few hundred persons heard five lectures on "Philosophy as a Way of Life" at the Chicago Art Institute in the spring of 1929. Some came to pray and went away to scoff; some came to scoff and went away to pray; some came sober and went away smiling; some came smiling and went away sober; some came wise and went away feeling foolish; some came foolish and went away feeling wise; many bore in silence whatever they bore; and some through discerning criticism helped those lectures to become this book, even as the antecedent interest and courtesy of Carl F. Huth, dean of the Downtown College of the University of Chicago, had helped part of this book to become those lectures.

Particularly you meet here, in the limbo of many a page, my scientific colleagues, George K. K. Link and D. Jerome Fisher, and pervasively here, as everywhere in my work, the genial presence and corrective touch of my most philosophic friend, Charner Marquis Perry. With these for real though invisible company, shall we now hazard the philosophic way? As you attend critically to each philosophic guide in turn, you may profit from the mellowed temper of Kipling's builder who in laying foundations for his own palace came upon the ruined grandeur of a forgotten king—

Lime I milled of his marbles; burned it, slacked it, and spread;
Taking and leaving at pleasure the gifts of the humble dead.
Yet I despised not nor gloried; yet, as we wrenched them apart,
I read in the razed foundations the heart of that builder's heart.
As he had risen and pleaded, so did I understand
The form of the dream he had followed in the face of the thing he had planned.

                                         T. V. S.

INDEPENDENCE DAY, 1929

CONTENTS

xiii

CHAPTER I

THE PHILOSOPHIC AND OTHER WAYS OF LIFE

Love but the formless and eternal Whole
From whose effulgence one unheeded ray
Breaks on this prism of dissolving clay
Into the flickering colours of thy soul.
Those flash and vanish; bid them not to stay,
For wisdom brightens as they fade away.

—SANTAYANA

THERE is no philosophy—only philosophers and their philosophies. Common to all philosophies past and present is the fact that they are ways of meeting life. They have served their makers usefully; otherwise they would not have been made. Since their makers have been men, the philosophies can presumably be of some service to other men. In detail there are as many ways of meeting life as there are men. To compress into classes, however, there are, above the bovine and the feline levels—neither of which is here recommended for either men or women—five major attitudes toward life: the *religious*, the *scientific*, the *social*, the *aesthetic*, and the *philosophic*. These do not entirely exclude each other, as we shall see; but the classification will prove useful and will be so qualified as not to be misleading. It is the cause of the philosophic way that we are to plead; but our plea is to be through example and insinuation rather than through proof and disproof. Indeed, the differences among the five ways had best be thought of as family differences and come at in genial mood. We shall strive to discover and to conserve whatever of worth there may be in each of them rather than ruthlessly to push the philosophic way to glory over the remains of the others. If we can succeed at this method, we shall in the sequel enrich life rather than merely feed the pride of professional philosophers.

Let us start with the factual observation that men are the kind of animals that do have ideas. Something can be reasonably said as to the circumstances under which ideas arise, since no one thinks all the time about any one thing. Ideas arise when and where neither the impulsive thrust nor the habitual mechanism of man suffices for the satisfaction then demanded. Ideas at their simplest are pictures not of things as they are, but of things as they might be if they were more satisfactory than they actually are. It is the fact that things are unsatisfactory that produces in ideas improved patterns for reality. In some idyllic heaven there would be no occasion for ideas, for thinking. Ideas always have at least as their fringe some improvement of existing circumstances. Since this fringe has no hard reality to answer to, it is subject to further inquiry. Indeed, ideas themselves become a problem to us; we get ideas regarding the meaning of ideas. Philosophy concerns itself in general with an understanding and criticism of the rôle of ideas in life. Since all the ways here considered are idea-ways, they are all in some basic sense philosophic ways of life. What constitutes *the* philosophic way of life we mean to indicate as sequel to the discussion of the foregoing major attitudes.

Three interpretations of ideas as such present themselves at once. The first arises from the fact that we have been born of, reared by, and conditioned to people. The forces that we first knew were personal forces that ministered to our needs. Our long infancy set this first discovery into a veritable law of nature for us. When in difficulty hunt a person to help: this is the summarized moral of human experiences in infancy and childhood. Little wonder, then, that when the colossal discrepancy that adolescence reveals between the needs arising from glandular pressure and satisfactions reserved for adults drives us to dreams, we create a world of people who understand our needs and who would help us to their satisfaction. If our need be critically great, we cling avidly to personages born of the race's adolescence and preserved by its pathetic credulity to succor our weakness with their great power. Thus gods are made, and angels that attend them, and fairies that flit about the world to inform children of the magic that lies at the heart of things. In this wondrous land

> the pipe is heard
> Of Pan, Invisible God, thrilling the rocks
> With tutelary music, from all harm
> The fold protecting.

Out of the most crucial human needs ideas arise personified into power, and ideas that arise from needs less pressing are assimilated to these as means of grace. The whole life of mind becomes the machinery of salvation from a world that produces more desires than it can naturally satisfy. Men set their affections on things above rather than on things on the earth. The marked susceptibility of adolescence to religious conversion renders plausible this interpretation, and the almost universal necessity for adults to look back to adolescence to quicken their religious devotion corroborates this account. We come back thus from one interpretation of the meaning of ideas to the religious way of life.

But if childhood has been happy and adolescence passes without too many frustrations, either one of two other interpretations of ideas may arise. If one's life has been easy, if leisure has been abundant, if wants have been satisfactorily supplied by others, and if the passing hours have thus been their own reward, one is likely to emerge treating ideas for what they seem to be—bright playfellows on the surface of the stream that bears both men and thoughts upon its placid bosom. Too sophisticated to treat personifications as powers, too independent of circumstances to be forced to treat them as plans for improved action, such a person takes them gratefully as constituting a beautiful world all their own, and, as Elizabeth Barrett Browning said of her childhood,

lives with dreams instead of with men and women.

The aesthetic way of life is an idea-way to happy souls harmoniously nurtured and materially subsidized.

Most men, however, are not above economic want and, partly because of this, are not harmoniously nurtured. They live by their wits. The necessity that prompts this indicates another interpretation of ideas. Ideas can be used as instruments of adjustment, and if successfully used they can make less poignant the dissatisfaction that generates them. The majority of men cannot afford luxuries, and so ideas must be exploited for their utility rather than for their admitted beauty. A man must live before he can live well; and most of life for most men is taken up with making a precarious living. Thinking is thus made to fertilize action, and the naturalization of ideas in the alien world that produces them is held to be the chief duty of man, because it is his only salvation.

This is the scientific way of life come to full fruition.

I

Of these three basic attitudes, religion represents the most ancient and the most common. It is the easy way. It has appeared to many the royal road. While as a road it has sometimes been criticized as leading not into but out of life, it has been defended by its devotees as leading from a meager life into a life more abundant. We take as the heart of religion what is common to all its forms and emphasize its practical significance as a way of facing life. All religions, like Christianity, began as a way whereby men sought to improve their lot.

The way is in essence a short-cut to satisfaction. Art is long, time is fleeting, life is hard. If men have to go the long way of discovering concrete means and adapting them to ends, they will never live long enough to achieve the ends felt necessary to prevent life's losing its deepest significance. One result of this easy, though terrible, discovery is to despair of life on earth, interpret it as a pilgrimage, and seek through complete renunciation here complete felicity elsewhere.

Gods grow up as a guaranty that goodness will not remain wholly impotent in a world of hostile powers. Another result of this discovery is to resort to symbols as means to power. In primitive religions there are effigies, idols, fetishes by manipulation of or attitude toward which present objects serve as controls for absent ones. In more developed religions, belief in God, or wholehearted acceptance of his messenger, Jesus or Joseph Smith, Mohamet or Mary Baker Eddy, or the saying of prayers in the right form and spirit, or the performance of penance, or the perpetration of pilgrimages is counted for righteousness' sake; and by belief or demeanor men lay hold upon desired ends. Symbolic acts that come easy substitute for the natural means that come hard, if at all. Religion does indeed invent powers and persons to validate this substitution. Of course a man's reach should exceed his grasp, or what's imagination for? But the basic thing, because out of it these arise, is the disposition to will the easy way to be the real way to success. In some "sign" the religious person always conquers—if conquer he does.

> . . . . from these create he can
> Forms more real than living man,
> Nurslings of immortality.

If the redoubtable walls that guard life's treasures are too strong for our actual engines of attack, then let us march around them the right number of times, in the right formation, and blow the right number of blasts upon the right horns. Have faith, and down they tumble. If works won't, then faith will.

Religion might survive the death of all the gods; but when men cease to believe in a short-cut, religion is no more. This is the minimum distinction that can serve to clarify rather than to mystify, to rectify rather than merely to perpetuate obsolescent boundaries. There might be science or art or philosophy but not religion. Religion is the readiest response of impotence to imposing power. Some religious persons will object to our definition as being invidious. It is admitted that definition may be used to create, to perpetuate, or to annihilate. If, however, we permit professionally religious people to define religion, then its future is as secure as their sinecures. To their objections, our reply must be Thomas Hobbes' cryptic remarks upon certain of his critics. "These things," he said, "I have found most bitterly excepted against: That I made the civil powers too large, but this by ecclesiastical persons. That I had utterly taken away liberty of conscience, but this by sectaries. That I had set the princes above the laws, but this by lawyers."

Of course there is no law against the vague use of terms. Temperaments differ here, and each has its rights. The term religion is, admittedly, used now to cover anything and everything. But straw is not grasped by the lusty swimmer. The avidity of pious persons for making everything religious has developed with the loss by religion of any specific and indubitable content of its own. When people really believe in God, they have something specific to call religious, and so do not need to describe scientific experimentation, or secular philanthropy, or aesthetic enjoyment as religion. There are other terms available, and historically sanctioned, to describe the latter activities. It represents verbal economy and mental clarity to surrender terms when their normal meaning and natural content is gone. There is of course always a reason why men are not willing to make this surrender. Basically it is the emotional satisfaction that comes from maintaining old attitudes regardless of whether they are rationally justified or not. Men crave the satisfaction of primitive beliefs long after the beliefs themselves are renounced. Clearly the use of religious categories to describe attitudes and activities already better described by other terms is such a surreptitious quest for satisfaction. But it is so common as to be respectable; there is no law against it; and there must be tolerance for it. That it serves a rôle one can observe in his nearest neighbor, if indeed he need to look beyond himself to observe it.

But with such tender-mindedness, such satisfying puzzle-headedness, we need not here concern ourselves. There *is* a religious way of life, with a legitimate historical content, a way of life well described by sacred categories and not well described by any other; and it is this that we have been meaning to make clear. It has a past, it has a present, it will have a future. Its utility one may judge for himself when its description is rendered unambiguous. There remains over and above science and art and philosophy the way of faith, the will to depend upon a short-cut to success in the venture of life. This is religion. Scratch the skin of the most liberal person in the world; and if he call himself religious, some germ of this attitude will be found. It is this germ that makes him religious. When he loses this germ, he ceases to call himself religious and contents himself with more direct and straightforward discourse. It is only when men know not what to trust that they trust they know not what.

When there were no telephones and no doctors, men depended upon prayer to heal the sick. That was religion—the use of words and gestures, when they did not know what else to use to achieve their ends. But when doctors are near and telephones at hand, the use of the telephone to summon the doctor is not called a religious exercise— except by apologists. The presence of adequate natural means removes any given field of life from the realm of religion in all plain talk; and the natural history of religion in civilized times is a gradual surrender of province after province of its ancient realm to art, to philosophy, but most of all to science. What prevents the completion of this recession is (1) grossly unequal distribution of economic goods and (2) uncertainty of the cosmic weather.

Even in periods, like our own, of great per capita wealth, poverty persists for the majority of people. In a wage and price economy, unemployment constitutes real poverty; and there is no great nation today whose unemployment does not permanently stand in seven figures—ten million in Western civilization continuously unemployed. But where absolute poverty stares a small percentage in the face at any given time, relative poverty remains hungrily near the door of more than half the world's population. For poverty cannot be accurately described except in terms of the discrepancy between goods visible and those available. Even in America, now most favored in this regard, substantially more than half the population has a money income adjudged by every impartial and humane agency that has surveyed the facts to be insufficient to satisfy those human wants whose satisfaction constitutes civilization. Under capitalism inadequacy of income means the proportionate denial of all other goods. For the poor, health remains relatively insecure; and opportunities at education, at culture, at self-development depend largely upon economic means. Where the will to live remains active, it always has constituted its own ideas into magic means, if actual economic means could not by any effort be secured. If the poor remain always with us, then religion's future is secure. Prosperity is rightly feared by the pious. Where poverty prevails, religion remains the only confirmation of the ancient and pathetic faith that good men at last get the goods.

> I preached passionately
>   That the meek shall inherit the earth,
> And that of the poor is the kingdom of heaven,
> And that the last shall be first,
> And that woe shall come to him who harms the
>   least of these.
>
> For I was of the lowly,
> And I was poor,
> And I was the last,
> And I was of the least of these.

The insecurity, moreover, that haunts the poor save as they are desensitized by a powerful religious faith is not unknown among those better to do. The economic structure of modern civilization, especially the crucial credit system, has outgrown the understanding of it, and consequently is dogged by the fear that follows suspected, even if not admitted, impotence in the face of important change. Moreover, the so-called economic laws constitute but a part of the environment on whose drift all things human necessarily attend. Human control over even things human in origin is not sufficient to satisfy men with the merely empirical; and the boundary of the very largest control is far this side of what we glimpse to be the potencies of this unbounded universe. Because man's life and hope is a hazard in this vast disarray which is the world, religion persists to encourage faith in efficacy of means other than natural causal agencies.

The universality and inexorability of this hazard is nowhere more fully attested than by the fact of death. The same impetus that leads men in quest of goods that satisfy their wants demands an indefinite continuation of the wants and their satisfaction; and the potency of this urgency to guarantee the goods prevails to demand the continuation of life itself. Death would mark the ruin of creative imagination were the imagination not able to triumph over it. To guarantee that all its other guaranties will not count for naught religion must deal with death in an heroic manner. The cosmic uncertainty here becomes a certainty for the worst, except as

> the worst turns the best to the brave

and religious affirmation triumphs over natural frustration.

These observations upon the vitality of the religious attitude but serve to reveal its essence. The poor man's hope that he will at last get the goods depends not on foresight of means that will bring him to fortune but upon faith in some technique that circumvents the hard means that have reduced him to poverty. A hopeful report upon the cosmic weather can be had only by manipulating the charts, not by scanning the stormy skies. And a

> faith that looks through death

is not the natural child of years that bring the philosophic mind. To think that the wanting of something strongly enough by somebody is guaranty that it will be had is to prove oneself potentially religious; and to depend upon means other than the natural common ones to bring to pass the desired end is in practice to live life religiously. To believe that there is an easy way out of all the hardest difficulties of life is to be religious: and since nobody becomes an adolescent without first having been a child, or an adult without having been an adolescent, the future of religion is hardly in doubt. Grave difficulties and hazards are likely to dog to the end the course of human life.

II

If to live life religiously is to constitute ideas into guaranties that short-cut means will actually work, then to live life aesthetically is to take ideas for their own sake, to take them as ends rather than as means. In the adventure which ideas constitute, there are distinguishable stages. Something always goes before ideas and something always comes after them. They may be conceived as arising from some portion of what goes before and as leading up to some portion of what comes after. They may thus be thought of as effects of prior circumstances, or they may be described as the causes of what comes after them. Or they may be isolated in the stream of circumstances on which they ride and, taken just for what they are, be made objects of attention and of admiration. Foregoing the gentle joys of memory and the livelier joys of imagination, one may contemplate the passing show as a show and pronounce it good. Religion, as we have seen, makes powers and even persons of ideas. Indeed it projects them into a realm of their own and reorients life with reference to them, rather than uses them merely for the enrichment of that segment of life in which they arise. The aesthete does nothing to the passing pageant save to observe and to enjoy it. It is its own reward. "Born of suspended attention," as Santayana says, "it ends in itself."

It is clear that this is not so simple, not so easy, not so materialistic a way of life as that which religion exemplifies. It implies a power of abstraction that is much more difficult to achieve than the simple and indigenous power of hypostatization or of personification upon which religion relies. It implies a refinement of taste to catch the rarefied and the attenuated. And, altogether, it implies a disciplined imagination—disciplined to detect and arrest the ideational aspect of experience and disciplined to forego the animal propensity of making ideas agencies to thicken and to insure experience. If, as a certain philosopher has said, "things are what they are and not another thing," then ideas and symbols, too, may be enjoyed for themselves without backward or forward glances. To concentrate one's energies in the present, keeping up with it as it flows and thus taking up the slack between understanding and feeling—this is to regard life aesthetically. To be an aesthete means to enjoy the present so much as to become immune to lessons taught by experience and to disavow responsibility for future consequences of present enjoyment. "The purely aesthetic observer," as Irwin Edman remarks, "has for the moment forgotten his own soul, and has gained the world, that is to say, the world of art." To rationalize this practical attitude into a general view that ideas have no history and have no consequences but are alone what merely they seem to be in passing—this is to become a philosopher with an aesthetic nucleus to one's system. As far as this is permanently possible, one can make life "a continuum of roses and raptures." Moreover, one may then live in the beautiful faith proclaimed and practiced by Santayana that "the happy filling of a single hour is so much gained for the universe at large" and that to find joy and self-sufficiency in the flying moment is perhaps the only means open to us for increasing the glory of eternity.

III

Science may have had its birth in wonder, as the ancients said, but not in wonder about things in general. The presence of practical difficulties which must be met before men can be comfortable and happy has always marked the locus of the wonder that produces science. Geometry is said to have arisen from the need of remarking land boundaries after successive inundations of the Nile, and all mathematics has been at least in its initial stages tied up with the resolution of practical needs. Science is indeed but the systematic and foresighted way mankind has developed for meeting the difficulties that beset it. Its cue is the understanding of nature; its objective and justification is control of natural processes for human ends. To make the scientific attitude a way of life is to become emotionally wrapped up in the process of understanding and controlling the course of nature. This tends strongly, as we shall later see, to pass into an aesthetic outlook upon natural events and processes.

The scientific way of life differs from the religious way in confining itself to the realm of nature. It does not seek short-cuts to control, save as natural means can be empirically telescoped through invention. The long way is the short way because it is the only way. If cancer is making inroads on human life and relief is sought, then the only scientific way of taking the matter is to find out the cause, isolate it, learn its ways, its antidotes, and then immunize human beings to it through the knowledge thus laboriously and haltingly acquired. Prayer will not help, faith in nothing will help, except such faith in the efficacy of human intelligence, ingenuity, and effort as will keep one unfaggingly at the job. Nor, pending success, will the universal religious expedient help—the expedient of believing that what man seems helpless before must somehow be for the best. No great religion but has encouraged resignation in the face of baffling evils. It is true that this encouragement proceeds upon the assumption that human insight is fallible and that if the evil could be truly seen it would be seen to be better than it seems. But this very assumption tends to make a virtue out of ignorance and thus to discourage the maximum effort at enlightenment. To call somehow good that which plain common sense reveals to be unmitigatedly bad is to stultify discrimination and to dull sensitivity. The scientific temper will see no reason why men should change their judgment of evil just because it as yet baffles control: to do so removes the necessity of control. To the scientific mind there is really nothing to be done about such things except to learn what they are and to get rid of them. The whole matter is simple in statement, difficult in achievement. But there is no substitute for doing the job if there is a job to be done.

The scientific way of life differs from the aesthetic way through its emphasis upon the interrelatedness of things. The aesthetic person can regard each object or experience as standing on its own base, as being what it is, and as borrowing nothing, giving nothing. The scientist cannot. He knows that nothing exists without a cause, not even the cause itself; and since things are tied together in sequences, he must know the earlier if he hopes to control a later stage of this flowing reality that passes before his eyes. Nothing is self-sourced; everything appears to be system-sourced. Nothing can take the place of knowledge of the system in which a given event occurs if we wish to deal effectively with it. What is true of things is equally true of ideas. *Ex nihil, nihil venit.* Ideas do not spring out of the blue; they are the effects of occurrences. It is indeed only through counting them as integral links in a chain that we can use them—as use them we do—to direct our course among things. Instead therefore of ideas being something whose significance is contained in themselves and appropriated by contemplation, their significance is really found in that to which they point and is appropriated never by contemplation but always by manipulation of the process so as to decrease the unwanted, increase the wanted, elements of the series to which they belong. They do not serve science who only stand and stare.

The scientific way of life, therefore, counts ideas as results of past events and treats them as predictive of future events. They thus become instruments of human improvement. This attitude implies a modesty and a patience and a sympathy that neither of the foregoing ways of life requires. A sympathy for other men means not merely that we feel with them but that we take their feeling at its face value. To ask one to enjoy his suffering as a passing phase of a perfect world is not sympathy. To counsel patience under remediable handicaps and suffering is not ethically plausible. Patience becomes of value only when it means fruitful forbearance under difficulties that are being solved in the only way that really eliminates them. Without this virtue scientists would never build on one another's shoulders for eventual conquest of what is always pressing upon man's spirit. They would take the short-cut offered by religious faith, and manipulate some more available substitute means in the hope that thus the end could somehow be achieved. Either contemplation or resignation is easier than mastery through effective manipulation. Modesty shows itself in the acceptance by the scientist of the general framework of the world as he finds it. It might have been different and better, but after all it is as it is. If it is now to be made better, its improvement must come about through the exploitation of resources that are observably in it.

The only resources for improvement that are indubitably available are human ideas of improvement and human ingenuity for effecting it. There may be a God; there are men. God may be good; men do have ideas of improvement. Faith and prayer might do some good; intelligent work will do the job. Intelligence may come to him who waits and hopes; ideas do come to him who subjects himself to difficulties and keeps his mind open. Himself a part of the universe, the

scientist cannot reprobate it without sham-
ing himself; but having in himself the power
of judging its processes differentially he cannot be true to himself without working to
make his own interests triumph in a cosmos
that seems oftentimes indifferent to them.
Taking himself for better rather than for
worse, he finds his vocation in enlarging his
sphere of influence. The scientific mind ex-
ploits history to enlighten the present; it
uses the present to improve the future. The
scientist knows that contemplation leaves
things precisely as they were, and that short-
cuts are gold bricks that coin nothing but
counterfeit.

IV

There is moreover another speculative
way of looking at and living life. It grows
out of an emphasis upon people as being the
most important material in the world, in the
formation even of one's own personality. We
know as a matter of simple observation that
some people get more ideas and better ideas
than do others. We know that this potency
is determined, as we say, by how sensitive
the person is. We know, furthermore, that
the sensitizing of a human being goes on

largely in terms of his social contacts, his companionships. Even though we regard ideas as the most important thing in the living of life, we should be thrown back to emphasize greatly the importance of the social environment in which one lives.

If, in addition to holding that it is the presence and influence of other people upon one that determines his capacity for ideas, we believe that the sheer enjoyment by man of other men constitutes a very great good in life, we should then be obliged to hold the social element in human life to be a determining emotional factor as well as intellectual influence. Feeling this way, one might easily come to believe that the end of life for any human animal is the enjoyment of his fellowmen and that the way of making the most out of life is the production of a fruitful social environment which in turn will produce such ideas, such science, such philosophy as will re-fertilize the social process itself. This attitude would explain ideas as being the products of human contacts and would clarify their functions as the making of human relations more beautiful.

What is necessary to make this a thoroughgoing and complete way of life is the belief that human personality itself is in very truth the result of social factors. It is an old and simple view of human nature which conceives it as being tied up with a soul, a soul that at some definite time comes to inhabit the body and direct its course, making possible ideas, emotional experiences, and all that we know of as best in human life. On such a view society comes to be a collection of these independent and metaphysically separated souls. Marriage is the sacrament of fusion; business in the meeting of minds through contract. Another view of this whole matter, however, has become prominent in our time. In simple form it holds that while we are born organisms, we do not have at first or acquire at any stated time a soul. A soul is an achievement, a growth, a product of our contacts with other people. Men are born animals, they grow to be human. The simplest explanation of how this comes about is speech. The human species is born with a mouth and a flexible tongue and grows upright with two free hands to carry things so that the mouth may be constantly used for its social purposes, that is of emitting sounds. We have ears to hear the sound given forth by other mouths, and eyes to see the objects to which other people point while they are making sounds. In this way we acquire the first rudimentary material out of which to construct our own speech. It has meaning to others since we have borrowed it from them, and it comes to have the same meaning to us that it has to them. Moreover, we can hear with our ears what our own mouths say, and when we come to say to ourselves the same thing that the sound says to other people, we have acquired consciousness, yea, self-consciousness. Out, therefore, of the ready device of speech, based upon the principle that anything may come to mean anything else if it be strategically associated, we build a personality and acquire intelligence.

It is, of course, not strange that if this be the way we come by our personalities, our personalities would find their use and joy in contributing to the process which gives them their birth and maintains their integrity. This process, I repeat, is social life, our contacts with other people; and out of it there arises and into it there goes back as material all the intelligence which we as individuals possess. The meaning of all our terms and even of our pretentious scientific and philosophical categories is a meaning borrowed from, and should eventually contribute to, the social process. If these be the facts, then one cannot avoid social responsibilities. He cannot run away from the group because, as Emerson said, "when me they fly, I am the wings." His very soul is born of the group, is constituted by the group, and the total feeling and value and joy of his life must be found in humble recognition of the social origin and in responsible discharge of the duties which are thus laid upon him. To see the full reach and significance of this explanation constitutes what is here described as the social way of life. Indeed it furnishes a goal for science conceived as power. It explains the religious and aesthetic motifs in life, explains the one so as to transcend it, the other so as to appropriate it.

V

Ideas may, then, be held to have their meaning in a higher realm of persons and powers to which they point, or in themselves, or in the world of things and natural processes for which they mark the way to improvement, or in friendship and social co-operation as the final goal of human life. To see each of these as *a* philosophic way of life is itself the beginning of *the* philosophic way of life. Each of them, as we have noted, consti-tutes an idea-way; each of them arises nat-urally and psychologically from describable sets of circumstances confronted by life in this actual world. The philosophic way of life par excellence is not merely, however, to discover that each of them is a philosophic way but to see that each of them is a product at various stages of a continuous single proc-ess. That is, the first function and service of the philosophic way of life as such is to be-come wise in the way of ideas and sympa-thetic with the needs that ideas serve. To deny religion to a man who has not and can-not get access to any other idea-way is to condemn to the bovine level a creature with the potentiality of a philosopher. To deny aesthetic enjoyment to him who has it and can afford it is to impoverish what is richer without our meddling. To discourage the utilization of ideas for the control of nature and the amelioration of human ills is not a task worthy of a philosopher. To see life steadily should result in helping to keep it whole. No ideas that arise from natural circumstances and no attitude toward them is to be denied its right by the philosopher except as he can modify circumstances and furnish foundation for a better way of life.

But the last qualification opens the way for the philosopher to be also a man. It goes without saying that a philosopher who is also a man is better than one who is just a philosopher. A philosopher may be as impartial as a mirror, but a man must have his preferences. Preferences may be assets where openly avowed. My own preference for the scientific way of life constitutes for me the philosophic way of life. The use of the definite article in the title of this book does not imply that my preference is the only one that can be described as philosophic, but it does imply that I think it the best one. Let me extract the fangs of this dogmatism by beginning at once to explain and justify my preference.

Certain negative grounds for this preference have already emerged. Implicit in what

I have said about the aesthetic way of life is
the critical fact that historically and actually it has been available to only a few people.
This might constitute no valid objection to
it if wrapped up in its vitals were seeds of
dissemination. Exactly the opposite seems
to be true. No way is known to increase the
brightness of life except to utilize ideas for
control. The fact that we trust chance only
when we can do nothing else shows that we
expect from it no great good. The aesthetic
way of life sterilizes ideas of their potency
for good by regarding them as impotent in
action, however beautiful in being. At best
the contemplation of them leaves the world
for others precisely as it was; at worst, it
leaves it very much poorer than it might
have been had the energy given to contemplation been turned to reconstructive use.
Implicit in what we have said about the religious way of life is the same moral. In so
far as all people are led to accept this way of
life—and to proselyte has been the bounden
duty of most religions—life on earth remains
as much poorer as the energy thus spent
might improve it if spent otherwise.

To take these, however, as the last word

would show us scientific zealots indeed. But they are true as far as they go. And they go far to indicate that what makes them possible as ways of life is the fact that not everybody travels them. The taking of life scientifically by the majority of men makes it possible without dire tragedy for a minority to take life in these other fashions, precisely as the fact that the majority of men work makes it possible for the few to combine leisure and luxury. The exploitation of ideas for their utility by producers and traders has kept the body of grosser goods—food, clothing, and shelter—sufficient to save from starvation and cold the religious as they journeyed through this world to a better and the aesthetic as they dallied in enjoyment of the scenery along the way. The scientific attitude toward ideas is the only attitude capable of being generalized to include all men. This is one high recommendation of it and the basic justification for our preference in its favor. It is a recommendation higher still when it calls the social way to be its end and the aesthetic way to be its crown. If it is not only capable of being generalized but can be made to include, as well as tolerate, the other attitudes, then it stands positively indicated as the preference of all thoughtful men.

That it can be thus justified represents our major conviction. But so to justify it confesses that there are genuine values in the other attitudes toward life, even though they have not shown themselves heretofore available to all men. Whatever sacrifices we may make of their values to include them in the scientific purview and thus put them within reach of all men would not be without its compensations. To this task we shall set our hand in the last chapter, after we have explored more fully the significance of each of these ways of life as seen in a distinguished American example.

Let us in now recalling what has been said anticipate more fully what we shall discover to be the feel of the philosophic way of life.

To take life philosophically is to take it with all the help others can give but at last to take it boldly upon one's own. It is to rest in the faith that since man has a head it is better to use it; it is through the complete mastery of the ideational process to leave no ideas unappropriated for life; and it is through a frank recognition of the wants of men as constituting the ends for which we live to count all men into the social enterprise that ideas serve either as art or as science. It is to tread the threefold path of wisdom: to know what one wants, to discover how to get it, and then to learn to want what one gets. It is to accept uncomplainingly what all must accept, but what many men accept complainingly. It is to live in the light of distant stars remembering with a long eye for history the contributions that other men and times have made and foreseeing with a quickened imagination the judgments of generations yet to come upon our workmanship. It is to think as clearly, to feel as sensitively, to share as sympathetically as our limitations allow, and to hold and to proclaim the faith that what is true and good and beautiful for one may become so for others. It is to act upon the presumption that what of good may be, should be. So to be and so to live is, we shall see, to exemplify in finest fashion the philosophic way of life.

CHAPTER II

THE RELIGIOUS WAY OF LIFE WITH JOSIAH ROYCE AS GUIDE

A hidden light illumes all our seeing,
  An unknown love enchants our solitude,
We feel and know that from the depths of being
  Exhales an infinite, a perfect good.

—SANTAYANA

WHATEVER men in general may think of philosophy, the philosopher regards his insight as a superior way of living. It is a way of thinking, to be sure; but thinking arises from and contributes to life. The final justification of his way of thought to the philosopher is that it facilitates his living as well as his thinking. What helps him—so he is committed to think—will help others. As recondite as will appear to some the philosophy we are to examine in this chapter, it was in the estimation of its author an exemplification of the foregoing remarks. Our present guide indeed defines philosophy as the attempt to find out what, on the whole, "experience is and means." "That all our beliefs about truth of any grade and that all theories have a practical meaning I do indeed explicitly teach. That, in fact, as my reader will see, is my whole philosophy."

Such a person, then, furnishes the nucleus of our present discussion. It is very fitting that our consideration of the religious way of life should be bound up with a person. Religious men have frequently cited the embodiment of religion in personalities as one of its advantages over philosophy austere in its presumed impersonality. While we deny this imputation upon philosophy, we are pleased nevertheless to put at the heart of this discussion a robust and lovable person— Josiah Royce. That he is a modern person is our good fortune; for the typical religious preference for some legendary far-away person, saintly in his isolation, is but pathetic naïveté. The only credible reason why a remote and dead man could be thought wiser and better than a modern is that the former has not had as good a chance to be found out. Piety by presumption is always precarious. We speak here of one we know; it is far more difficult but certainly much more significant to have faith in him as a guide. That he was a learned person is rare good fortune. The inheritance by our complex and industrial civilization of spiritual heroes simple in moral nature, benevolent in intention, but ignorant of the world of nature, and indifferent to natural knowledge suggests tragedy as well as wonder. Neither Royce's spirituality nor his predilection for metaphysics prevented his seeing the importance of science and social engineering, as witness his fine essay at the end of his life on social insurance.

Able to give a reason for all the faith that was in him, Josiah Royce spent his life in making clear to himself why he had elected the course he did take and in recommending his way of life to others. That his speculation constituted light upon his path, we cannot doubt. Whether it constitutes light upon our paths is for us to judge. Some men inherit a marked road to success; some have an itinerary thrust upon them; but Royce achieved his orientation through fervent travail. His philosophy is the record of this travail, and—let us assume as an experiment

—is appropriable by whoever will appropriate it. The problems that life posed for him are the central perplexities of the religious consciousness. It is not merely his problems, however, that make him a typical religious guide, nor yet the fact that he answers his basic questions as he does; it is also the total attitude he takes toward his problems and toward life that makes him a fair and fit nucleus for our evaluation of the finality of the religious way of life. We can perhaps do no better than to unfold our discussion around his problems: the possibility of knowledge, the nature of the natural universe, the problem of evil. Brooding over all is what perhaps we cannot catch, except by reading him for ourselves, a sense of the tragedy of man as he quests for salvation.

I

Temperamentally unadapted to take life aesthetically, Royce could not content himself with looking upon ideas as mere beautiful playthings, nor as eternal essences majestic in their isolation from minds human and divine. Nor could he conceive of their meaning as exhausted in themselves. Born in a western mining town, subjected in his nurture to an environment in which only those succeeded who knew how to do things, and they subject to many hazards, this philosopher early saw and came deeply to feel that ideas must be instruments of control if human life is not to be permanently impotent. But this implies that ideas must be true, that knowledge must be possible. Knowledge is possible only if ideas connect with something other than themselves. An idea is not of itself; and an idea that is merely of another idea is not knowledge. But can ideas be of anything beyond themselves? If they cannot, then knowledge is not possible for human beings; and if knowledge is not possible, then no assured control of nature is possible. Human life becomes as subject to hazards as is any other life, and as certain of eventual frustration. This is not a conclusion to be accepted as long as any other offers. The least that the ambitious mind can do is to exhaust all other possibilities before entertaining this conclusion.

Royce, our guide, stumbled hard upon this difficulty. It early came home to his honest soul that a final certification of virtue

should come from some source other than
the character in question. If ideas are to be
validated as representatives of a world other
than they, their proficiency should be certified by the world outside themselves. And
yet since it seemed clear to him that it is
through ideas that we know whatever we
know, how can it ever be clear that we know
anything except ideas? The ingenious ways
he had of stating this problem are almost as
interesting as his attempts at solution. John
and Thomas, as one illustration goes, fall
into conversation. They suppose themselves
to be alone; but it early appears that they
are not alone. For there figure into the conversation not merely John and Thomas, but
each one's idea of himself. This makes four
parties to the conversation. But almost at
once two other phantom parties appear—
each one's idea of the other. Two were company, but here's a crowd: the real John, his
idea of himself, and his friend's idea of him;
the real Thomas, his idea of himself, and his
friend's idea of him.

Only those who have not had misunder-
standings with their friends can suppose that
this analysis is wholly whimsical. He who

asserts that the three of each party boil down to one needs to indicate that this is true by showing *how* it can be made true. To put the matter at its simplest, one needs to know that his idea of himself is true, and this he cannot know without showing that his idea of himself is the same as himself. If it is difficult to know oneself, how much more difficult to know the real person back of our idea of the other man; and if this be difficult, how very much more difficult still it must be to know nature, speaking as she does so varied a language. Knowledge seems always to turn out to be of ideas, and to be inside our heads. What the ideas represent, we can never know; for they themselves are all we ever know about it. Since they are all we ever know, we do not know whether what they claim is true or not. With knowledge thus compromised, truth flees away; and with truth gone, man is left hugging his whims in the shadows of a portentous world.

Man's plight, as Royce in other mood explains it, is that of the medieval knights who meet by the side of a shield that is silver on one side and gold on the other. The one knight affirms it to be gold; the other swears it to be silver. They fight until sides are exchanged, whereupon each contradicts himself and affirms the other to be a liar. Life is a shield both sides of which—ideas and things—can never be glimpsed at once; and so we never know whether what we or others affirm to be true is true or not. We can fight and fall and die; but we cannot know. Since, however, knowledge is necessary for the safe conduct of life and certainly for our satisfaction in living it, we lack both safety and satisfaction. Reaching for these dear goods, we grasp only skepticism. Skepticism when finished brings forth pessimism, and pessimism when completed brings forth moral decay.

II

To accept as a fact the notion that men can never know anything except their ideas is very trying on flesh and blood. If it were not tragic, it would certainly be comic. That ideas, which exist to enable us to know other things, should stand in the way of our knowing anything but themselves would be a sardonic joke indeed for the most whimsical Olympians to play upon mortals. But men have entirely too much at stake to see this predicament in any comic light. That a man is shut up inside his own cave and the key thrown away is too much for Royce to believe. Perhaps some undisclosed notion about the nature of the world outside us makes possible the grim fear that we can never know reality as it is. We certainly do seem most naturally to assume that what we call the natural world is made up of material stuff wholly unlike what we believe our minds to be. Perhaps this is a false assumption. Since we can know ideas, if the outer world were such stuff as ideas are made of, then might we not know it and find ourselves able to control it for our own ends?

Royce does not proceed forthwith simply to assume that matter is a conglomeration of ideas and rest in that simple dogmatism. It is with dialectical ceremony and a sense of impending catastrophe or deliverance that he finally affirms the spiritual nature of reality. But to this grand affirmation he does finally come, and come with great relief. His first step in the direction is the discovery that the notion that the world is composed of hard alien matter is itself a

pure assumption. Common men accept all
too easily the fable of materialism. Scientific
men make this assumption to see what will
follow from it. The uniformity of nature is a
pure postulate of science, unproved and un-
provable. The truth is, says Royce, that if
he himself cannot know what reality is, nobody else can know. So others who claim to
know that it is material are out-talking their
information. They have sufficient reason, no
doubt, for believing it to be this or that. But
their reasons are not his reasons, nor his
reasons theirs. He claims as much right to
make an assumption as to the nature of the
universe as has any scientist; and he thinks
that he has a much better reason for his assumption. For he wishes a world that can
be known by science and common men alike.
They both assume a kind of world that he as
philosopher sees cannot be known by any-
body. He will assume a kind of world that
thereafter becomes knowable by everybody
alike. To assume a knowable world is better
than to assume an unknowable one. So exercising his right, he performs his duty; and,
lo, a world arises that since it is such stuff as
knowledge is can itself be known.

A world that is intelligible in texture would thus soften if not solve the problem of knowledge for one who starts with the notion that ideas are known. But such an interpretation of the universe does more; it does so much more in fact as to indicate that the problem of knowledge is preoccupation that conceals more important yearnings. Royce sees that scientists, regardless of their metaphysical inclinations, do ordinarily conceive the universe as intelligible. They not merely conceive it so by forming hypotheses which they expect to fit it; but they prove it so by verifying their hypotheses—verifying a far greater proportion of them, says Royce, than could be accounted for on any chance adaptation of mind to nature. The universe, then, is intelligible. Once this is concluded, it seems easy for most thinkers to pass to the notion that it is therefore intelligent. From a power that persons can understand and control, nature rises to the stature of a person whom one can trust and enjoy. From the notion that nature is rational (understandable by us) we pass imperceptibly to the notion that she is spiritual (understanding and sympathizing with us). There is another notion also that easily functions here, and does so in the case of Royce. Ideas are not usually thought of as floating about in empty space. They have their habitat in mind. Now when we make nature such stuff as can be understood, as is rational, as is ideal, it is easy to assume that the world of nature must therefore either be a mind or be in a mind. In either event, since nature is so gigantic, we get in her or encompassing her a majestic spirit.

Such a system of rationality conceived as encompassing us presents problems almost as grave as those it is supposed to solve. It is supposed to solve the major problem of making knowledge possible. It certainly does pose a major question of why human knowledge is necessary or even desirable. For a basic characteristic of knowledge is organization. The philosopher has a regular principle that he supposes to hold true of all minds: that one cannot believe a thing and its opposite at the same time. He calls it the law of contradiction. Whether it be literally true, we do recognize that in so far as a mind understands itself, it tries to make its ideas harmonious. Now a perfect mind would understand itself completely, even better than a psychanalyst could; and so in it there should not, it would seem, be any contradictions or tensions of any sort. In fact there should be in it perfect harmony, nothing needing to be otherwise. If nature be such a system, as Royce asserts, nothing in it is out of joint; and the simple notion with which Royce starts—that nature must be shown knowable in order to be rendered more amenable to our interests—is false. If nature is rational through and through, there is nothing for our minds to do, nothing needs doing, no knowledge is necessary. Contemplation, not knowledge, would be the outcome. All possible knowledge is already completely actual, for by definition everything is rational. Certainly there could be no necessity for converting into human knowledge what is already better knowledge and more complete harmony than human beings achieve. Knowledge if present at all becomes mere gazing; and control in the sense of changing anything becomes presumption if not impiety. A completely rational world has no place for the meddling mind of man. This is, however, perhaps not the most serious problem,

though perturbing enough itself. We have
been speaking of the rational system as being impersonal, as being harmonized relations and things. Once reach this conclusion,
why not go on? It is easy to pass from a rational impersonality to a sympathetic personality. Certainly Royce did so pass. With
such an outcome, a glorious vista unfolds before us to cover our problems with the
mantle of spirit.

Looking where our metaphysical guide
points, we see at the center of things a power
that is at the same time goodness. This is a
combination hard to achieve in human life.
It is our daily doom to feel ourselves helpless
against a nature of pitiless power. "The life
of man," as Bertrand Russell has it, "is a
long march through the night, surrounded
by invisible foes, tortured by weariness and
pain, towards a goal that few can hope to
reach, and where none may tarry long . . . .
for Man, condemned today to lose his dear-
est, tomorrow himself to pass through the
gate of darkness, it remains only to cherish,
ere yet the blow falls, the lofty thoughts that
ennoble his little day."

Though Royce knew from tragic experience what those words meant, he did not draw such a conclusion.

In the presence of what to him was essentially a tragic world, Royce achieves a faith "in the supremacy of the Good in this world of the Powers." If the power that is nature is really personal in character, then we can presume upon its benevolence. If this does not follow logically, it follows theologically. Good intention is so often unavailing in human life because good men do not have the goods and so are not able to make effective their yearnings. But good men may get the goods if there is both goodness and power at the heart of the universe. Since nature is perfectly rational and man is a part of her, he too must be perfectly rational. If the Absolute Spirit is really all in all, then human beings are but part of the supreme intelligence. Their thoughts are merely the thinking of his thoughts or else he is not the whole of nature. "The genuine God," as Royce says, is "no incomplete, struggling God, whom we might pity in his conflict with evil, but the all-embracing thought, in which the truth is eternally finished." In so far as a man thinks or otherwise experiences that which is less than the best, he is not having real experience at all. So at least it would appear, though it remained for Mary Baker Eddy unreservedly to draw this conclusion.

This problem of man's remaining man while achieving salvation in Absolute Spirit came weightily home to Royce, however; and to it his argument returns again and again. His greatest work, *The World and the Individual*, constitutes a frontal attack on this problem, though it is well to note that in the title the world precedes the individual. That the individual is real and important in the scheme of things Royce never doubts, but how to display and prove these theses was a never satisfactorily solved problem with him. The Absolute Spirit constitutes nature and involves us; its presence measures reality; and in it all contradictions are solved and harmony reigns supreme. Yet all is not well with the human spirit. We have our frustrations, our aches, our disappointments. It would seem necessary either to deny reality to these, as does Mary Baker Eddy, or admit the Absolute Spirit to be less than perfect. When face to face directly with the issue, Royce seems to incline to the latter view; for he insists that there is no humblest ache or pain that is not present to the Absolute. But when he describes the Absolute, with man for the moment forgotten, Royce beholds only perfection in which there is no variableness, neither shadow of turning. Human finitude fades from the picture. Since the Absolute is perfect, it might seem that man becomes real only in so far as he escapes the Absolute. Quite the opposite is true, according to Royce; for since the Absolute alone is real, man is real only as he finds his own individuality in that of the Absolute. Royce gives this old religious view a new life in a beautiful setting. Human beings achieve true individuality as they lose themselves in a cause. Loyalty is the last word of moral wisdom, and the final cause to which men must be loyal is loyalty itself. Here is indeed a way of life —a way in which all cues of conduct are caught from a source of superior insight, as all reality is imputed from higher to lower experience. But the problem of how there can be genuinely lower experience in a perfect world is one with which Royce wres-

tles manfully. It is in short the problem of
evil.

III

The Absolute Spirit which constitutes
everything else is perfect; but it constitutes
man a finite and imperfect creature. In an
atmosphere of perfection man suffers for his
imperfections. Why must he suffer? Is not
Almighty power lacking in goodness to permit other beings to be and to suffer from being less perfect than itself? Would perfect benevolence permit such to be if it had supreme
power? This age-old perplexity of the religious soul, felt by few saints more poignantly than by our philosopher Royce, can be
provocatively put by saying that God either
could have prevented evil and would not, or
would have but could not. If he could have
but would not, he is not altogether good; if
he would have but could not, he is not altogether powerful. Which horn of the dilem-
ma shall we choose—impotent goodness or
potent indifference?

Has some vast Imbecility,
  Mighty to build and blend,
  But impotent to tend,
Framed us in jest, and left us now to hazardry?

Or come we of an Automaton
   Unconscious of our pains? . . . .
   Or are we live remains
Of Godhead dying downwards, brain and eye now
    gone?

Or is it that some high Plan betides,
   As yet not understood,
   Of evil stormed by Good,
We the Forlorn Hope over which Achievement strides?

That the latter alternative points in the right direction Royce never doubted. He bent every energy to understand the "high Plan." His task of reconciliation was complicated in structure but facilitated in fact by his belief that since all that is enters into the experience of the Absolute Spirit, it enters all at once. Whatever was, always is; for there is no past and no future to Absolute Spirit. The Absolute's attention span is infinite. In short, time as we perceive it is unreal to the Absolute; and genuine change from worse to better (and of course from better to worse) is in reality impossible. There is indeed in a comprehensive view no better and no worse; for whatever is, is perfect in so far as it really exists. "To be," as Royce defines it, "is to fulfil purpose"; and fulfilment of purpose is assumed to be good. Otherwise the Absolute Spirit whose experience constitutes everything would not itself be perfect.

Since the Absolute is not in time (though time is in it), no evolutionary hypothesis is open to Royce as optimistic explanation how a perfect whole may be the outcome of imperfect parts. Organic evolution, like all temporal things, is a sort of byplay of the Absolute Spirit, a make-believe that what always has been is really for the first time coming to be. No soul clairvoyant with Absolute Being would for a moment be deceived by the play. To take the play for earnest is indeed not merely to lack discernment but to lack piety as well. To suppose that things can in their totality be made better by natural evolution or by human action reflects on deity who has already constituted them perfect in constituting them as himself. "Progress in this world as a whole is," as Royce says, "therefore simply not needed."

We must admit, with the religious in all ages, that this is to some extent a dark saying. But before leaving the question as to

why Eternal and Perfect Being as a whole
should be temporal and imperfect in its
parts, we must ask what is to be done about
it by us as parts? How can philosophy serve
as a guide to life? In spite of the absolute
irrelevance of action, we do and must act.
It is this corrective emphasis of Royce in the
face of his perfectionistic convictions about
reality as a whole that led George Santayana, his colleague at Harvard, to speak of
Royce's "double assurance that it was really
right that things should be wrong, but that
it was really wrong not to strive to right
them." Since, however, all is rational, thinking becomes the most important kind of action in the conduct of life. We are to live
life, even in the face of evil, by thinking
about it rightly. That is what we can do
about it, and that is enough. For if we once
see things truly, we shall see them to be
what they are—eternal and perfect in their
complete reach. So to see them is to achieve
the highest vision possible to man; it is to
achieve what Royce calls the "religious insight." For to be religious, as he conceives
the matter, is to perceive that what alone
conditions the reality of evil is the presence

and supremacy of good. This is, if true, so important a discovery that we ought to inquire how Royce reaches the momentous conclusion.

Looked at in the large, there are, he says, two kinds of evils: evils external to the will and evils inside the will. The first type he brushes aside in the conviction that we can never tell for certain whether the bad things that happen to us are really evil or not. We know that they sometimes turn out for our good. How do we know that they are not always for our own good if we could but see them and ourselves in the largest perspective? They may be evils merely by virtue of our ignorance. So we pass them by to consider the kind of evils that we know more intimately—the evils inside our own wills. That we do at times have an evil will, Royce admits. But when do we have an evil will? Not until we know that it is evil, or at least until somebody recognizes it for what it is. For to the man whose will is altogether evil his will does not appear evil at all. It takes a good man to know when he has done wrong. It takes a good will to reveal as evil the evil that is in it. Since, then, an evil will never appears evil save as it is over-topped by good, and since evil in the will is the least doubtful evil that we know—we may say that evil never appears except in a context of good. Encompassing good is thus disclosed as the necessary condition of evil; and evil by its very nature stands subordinated to its opposite.

Let us see clearly the logic by which Royce reaches this reassuring conclusion. Basic to his whole method is the notion that the meaning of anything is caught from its surroundings. Since Royce holds that meaning constitutes the nature of things, the nature of anything, as well as its significance, may be said to reside in a conscious context. Everything is what is is by virtue of its being included in something larger or higher. This is a principle in philosophy that is certified by age and by the deepest aspirations of men. It is at least as old as Plato, who seems to have believed that every specific thing is what it is by virtue of its "participating in," "partaking of," or "imitating" the class of which it is an example. He too used it eventually to subordinate all things else to a moral if not religious interpretation of the universe. Royce uses the logic not merely at the end of his philosophy but as a means to the end. He finds the deepest insight of morality in the discovery that the only condition on which skepticism is possible is a universality of faith. The logical insight, likewise, is the discovery that error is possible only because of the presence everywhere of absolute truth. In short, the existence of anything that one does not like proves the prior existence and the prevailing influence of everything that one does like. The religious insight is thus revealed as a happy ending of the whole career of mind; the motivation which successively through skepticism and error has made the better out of the worse, can at the end make from the worst the very best. The simple secret of all these several insights is that, in spite of first appearances to the contrary, the world is what we want it to be. And if it is, what more do we want?

To be religious, then, is precisely to see reality as it is—perfect. But the seeing has to be done against such odds that most men do not attain the insight. What must be changed to effect this happy ending is just oneself. Nothing is done to the world, but

to see it truly. Much must be done to oneself. Royce himself never succeeds exactly in
seeing the universe in its parts as wholly
good. What he does succeed in doing, however, is to believe that the whole is good in
spite of its parts. Great faith must therefore
supplement great speculative insight to make
life seem at the end of reflection what it
does not seem at the beginning of thought.
Royce pities those whose morale depends
upon an attempt to make the world a little
better day by day through their efforts. Not
that it may not be done. The career of
science and the resulting control over nature
show what can be done. But to depend upon
this piecemeal process for spiritual success is
the part of those with little faith. More can
be done for happiness in an hour of correct
thinking than in a year of scientific research.
Argument, dialectics is the shortest path to
spiritual power. The wise man does not depend, therefore, upon making nature better
day by day; he tries to make himself so
much wiser day by day that he can see the
world for what it is, absolutely good already.

In spite, therefore, of any notion that
may have developed that Royce's philoso-

phy was going to bring us a new way of uti-
lizing science for purposes of welfare, we see
that his central insight comes under the description of religion given in the first chapter. The religious way of life was there described as a short-cut toward ends the long
way to which was scientific and was un-
available for the immediate needs of many.
Royce's short-cut consists in manipulating
oneself rather than in correcting one's environment. Argument rather than industry
is the means. He supposes that the adverse
significance, if not the very reality, of things
bad can be remedied merely by our taking a
different attitude toward them; for bad
things seen truly *are* necessary constituents
of total and absolute good. The earlier examples given of the typical religious way of
life concerned prayer, magic, etc., practiced
upon an adverse environment. But to depend wholly upon one's attitudes or beliefs
or the process of dialectic is to invent in the
name of rationality a new magic, a short-cut
to success just as magical as the old. Its corollary is faith in a type of universe that despite all its elemental appearances subordi-
nates evils to good. We are here in the pres-

ence again of our elemental religious temper: if works won't, then faith will. When you see no other way to improve things, denounce the need to improve them, renounce the effort to do so; and, behold, the job is done. This is the royal road to such as find it possible. It encourages a renunciation of creative effort and a resignation to the order that already prevails.

IV

"A resignation to the order that already prevails." There's the rub. For the attitude that men finally develop toward the physical universe they will utilize toward the social universe. Religion has usually been regarded as a socially conserving agency. While it is not always so, it tends, when otherwise, to annihilate itself. This may be seen in the present plight of liberal Protestantism, whose fundamental perplexity is why it should continue to exist as religion. What as modernism it believes could as well be called ethics; what it feels could as well be called art; what it does could as well be called social service. Religion at its most typical is socially conservative because it ac-

cepts a given order and counts on changing
its adherents to fit the environment rather
than on adjusting the environment to the
individual. Herein lies what many feel to be
the greatest defect of the religious way of
life: its method of bettering life can never
transmit the improvements to others. Resignation breeds the necessity for resignation;
whereas environmental reconstruction trans-
mits the possibility of continued participation in and enjoyment of an improved world.

Royce accepted these liabilities and set
about to minimize them. Loyalty seemed to
him the final wisdom for the life of aspiration. Men are nothing in and by themselves.
The community's blood has gone into their
veins, and their thoughts are its intuitions.
The burden of the Pauline insight, argued
Royce, was this organic relation between the
individual and his community. Not good if
detached, this is the moral of man. His sense
of sin is but a confession of isolation, and the
experience of salvation is but a pean in honor
of belonging again. No man can be spiritually whole who is self-centered; for human
nature being in fact derivative finds its
health in acknowledging its dependence.

The most wholesome acknowledgment is found not in confession of sins but in devotion to a cause.

Philosophy for Royce precipitates as compound wisdom: *Find a worthy cause and be loyal to it unto death*. We have now only to apply to the quest for a cause the Roycean method as already developed, the method of hierarchical inclusion. Since nothing is real alone, the individual as such is illusory. The happiness of illusory beings is itself illusory. The individual will find his real happiness where he finds his true being —in something that includes him and is better than he is. This will be his cause. There are, however, many causes. How shall he choose among them? By the now familiar method: each cause must be judged by its being caught up in a larger and better whole, until at last the totality of things conceived as ideal, until at last the Absolute, until at last God stands revealed as both the source and the goal of life.

This is, again, the outcome of Royce's speculative system. His moral system ends in counseling loyalty to this. If the order of totality seems large, if the way to the Absolute seems vague because all ways are his ways, then God has not left himself without a witness. "Be loyal to loyalty," and there is no missing the way. If loyalty for its own sake seems abstract, then flee selfishness and know that in the loss of the finite, the true self will come to birth. Into enthusiastic prose Royce translates Emerson's poetic optimism:

> When the old world is sterile
>   And the ages are effete,
> He will from wrecks and sediment
>   The fairer world complete.
> He forbids to despair;
>   His cheeks mantle with mirth;
> And the unimagined good of men
>   Is yearning at the birth.

That there is in Royce's way of life fine feeling and great beauty and high significance no one can doubt. Even those who cannot take the road he points must admit, in the language of William James, that in contact with Royce one's "life is being lived significantly." Even though we ourselves shall have to let Royce go his way alone, we shall memorialize his psychological insight and human significance while traversing in chapter iv with another guide the social way of life. Royce leaves us at the boundary of the human community as he presses on to some "Great Community" that includes even humanity in its infinite folds. We bid him a fond farewell for what our limitations can but feel to be a fatuous journey. But we note the eagerness and confidence with which he pushes ahead, and we know that he has disclosed to us new meaning and potency in the community which we *can* comprehend. As for his religious faith, we can but say with Thomas Hardy:

> I am like a gazer who should mark
>   An inland company
> Standing upfingered, with, "Hark! hark!
>   The glorious distant sea!"
> And feel, "Alas, 'tis but yon dark
>   And wind-swept pine to me!"

We only know that Royce's method is important if correct, his assumptions marvelous if not fallacious. His method is the method of the religious in every age—*trust the bad to imply the good, the worse the better, the worst the best*. His assumptions are that evil stands subordinated to good rather than good to evil and that what men deeply dislike, what men desperately desire, can by logic be shown, respectively, not to be, and certainly to be, involved in the texture of reality. Let those who will and can follow this inspired guide

> On, to the bound of the waste,
> On, to the City of God.

As for us, we must at this juncture detour to take the scientific road.

CHAPTER III

THE SCIENTIFIC WAY OF LIFE
WITH WILLIAM JAMES
AS GUIDE

The salt, salt smell of the thick sea air,
And the smooth round stones that the ebbtides
    wear,—
When will the good ship come?

—SANTAYANA

WHAT way of life would we expect to be recommended by one who in his late twenties had such an experience as is poignantly described in the following narrative?

Whilst in this state of philosophic pessimism and general depression of spirits about my prospects, I went one evening into a dressing-room in the twilight, to procure some article that was there: when suddenly there fell upon me without any warning, just as if it came out of the darkness, a horrible fear of my own existence. Simultaneously there arose in my mind the image of an epileptic patient whom I had seen in the asylum, a black-haired youth with greenish skin, entirely idiotic, who used to sit all day on one of the benches, or rather shelves, against the wall, with his knees drawn up against his chin, and the coarse gray undershirt, which was his only garment, drawn over them, inclosing his entire figure. He sat there like a sort of sculptured Egyptian cat or Peruvian mummy, moving nothing but his black eyes and looking absolutely non-human. This image and my fear entered into a species of combination with each other. *That shape am I*, I felt, potentially. Nothing that I possess can defend me against that fate, if the hour for it should strike for me as it struck for him. There was such a horror of him, and such a perception of my own merely momentary discrepancy from him, that it was as if something hitherto solid within my breast gave way entirely, and I became a mass of quivering fear. After this the universe was changed for me altogether. I awoke morning after morning with a horrible dread at the pit of my stomach, and with a sense of the insecurity of life that I never knew before, and that I have never felt since. It was like a revelation; and although the immediate feelings passed away, the experience has made me sympathetic with the morbid feelings of others ever since. It gradually faded, but for months I was unable to go out into the dark alone.

In general I dreaded to be left alone. I remember wondering how other people could live, how I myself had ever lived, so unconscious of that pit of insecurity beneath the surface of life. My mother in particular, a very cheerful person, seemed to me a perfect paradox in her unconsciousness of danger, which you may well believe I was very careful not to disturb by revelations of my own state of mind. I have always thought that this experience of melancholia of mine had a religious bearing. . . . . I mean that the fear was so invasive and powerful that, if I had not clung to scripture-texts like *The eternal God is 'my refuge*, etc., *Come unto me all ye that labor and are heavy-laden*, etc., *I am the Resurrection and the Life*, etc., I think I should have grown really insane.

Whatever way of life we are to expect from such a character, if philosophy is to leave no ways of living unexploited, we are fortunate in being able to include among our guides one who has traversed the valley when the clouds hung low. Such a one was William James. The experience was his own, told in his own words, disguised as an anonymous Frenchman's, but later acknowledged to be of himself. From such a guide, it seems likely that we should expect recommendation of the religious way of life, since he himself attached religious significance to his experiences and since in it he received comfort from what are usually regarded as means of grace, scripture texts. There is ground for doubt whether this indicated conclusion follows, though there are to be found those who so argue. It at least follows that James could never so forget his experience as to be unsympathetic with religious people and unobservant of religious experiences. But this experience happened against a scientific background.

For already James was by training a scientist. Having turned in early manhood from painting as a possible career after a year's try at it in Paris, he devoted himself at Harvard to a mastery of science; chemistry first, then anatomy and physiology, and finally medicine in which at the very time of the experience he was engrossed. After a year as assistant to Agassiz on the Amazon and in Brazil, James said that this scientific association "so taught him the difference between all possible abstractionists and all livers in the light of the world's fulness, that he was never able to forget it." Though after his medical training was completed he did not elect to practice medicine, James nevertheless carried through life a flair for the concrete—a devotion to details, a curious, observant, and skilful eye—a physician's slant

among the metaphysicians.   Promissory of
what was to come, James as a scientific stu-
dent, before it was required or even expected
of him, made careful drawings of microscopic
observations in the laboratory at Harvard.
This background and training, when later
supplemented by the teaching of anatomy
and a rich apprenticeship in psychology, was
destined to make James the one outstanding
American recruit for the speculative enterprise from genuinely scientific preoccupation.

There was, moreover, another side to his
background—strangely enough, a religious
side—that weighted the scales in favor of a
scientific rather than a religious attitude. It
was his father, whom James believed to have
been the prime source of his intellectual life.
It is difficult to say whether his father was
theological without being religious or religious without being theological. The reader
may judge this for himself in the light of his
father's attitude. To the editor of the *New
Jerusalem Messenger*, an organ of the Sweden-
borgian movement to which the elder James
was once devoted, he wrote: "The old sects
are notoriously bad enough, but your sect

compares with these very much as a heap of
dried cod on Long Wharf in Boston compares with the same fish while still enjoying
the freedom of the Atlantic Ocean. . . . .
Your mature men have an air of childishness
and your young men have the aspect of old
women. . . . . It cannot but prove very un-
wholesome to you spiritually, to be so nearly
connected with all that sadness and silence,
where nothing more musical is heard than
the occasional jostling of bone by bone. Do
come out of it before you wither as an au-
tumn leaf, which no longer rustles in full-
veined life on the pliant bough, but rattles
instead with emptiness upon the frozen
melancholy earth." There is here none of
the thin-skinnedness and morbidity connoted by orthodox religion. As further earnest of his father's robustness, note the in-
structions he gave his daughter a week before his death to transmit to whoever con-
ducted his funeral: "Tell him to say only
this: 'Here lies a man who has thought all
his life that the ceremonies attending birth,
marriage and death were all damned non-
sense.' Don't let him say a word more!"

Though William James himself wrote a

book upon religious pathology and corre-
lated morbidities—in which the foregoing
experience of his own was included along
with the rest—he maintained always an
analytic technique, a good-humored manner,
and a general wholesomeness of curiosity,
which show that when he recovered from his
early sickness of soul, he actually recovered.
Never inclined to rear sickness into a norm
nor to claim to cure it by sanctimonious
short-cuts, he became early and remained
throughout life a vigorous exponent of
healthy-mindedness. I think the explanation lies in the influence upon him of this
wholesome family and scientific background.
It was this that prevented his original cure
from seeming to be effected through religious channels. Could he afterward have regarded his escape from insanity as a work of
grace—which his mention of scripture texts
has suggested to so many people—he would
in all probability have won the title he has
so widely received, a religious guide to life.
But as deep into the shadows as he pene-
trated, he did not go far enough to find God.
Of such a reality he always claimed, half-
regretfully, never to have had experience.

Nor did he go far enough to get esoteric intimations of immortality, nor any inside information on how men could be saved by other means than common sense and scientific insight. When he himself arose from the empty deeps—from which minds less virile would certainly have brought the authority of things seen and heard—he brought nothing save sympathy for those who suffer, and a scientific curiosity as to whether he would not have found something if he had gone further. He came back to health by empirical means, not by esoteric experiences. It was the reading of the poetry of Wordsworth, that ancient and wholesome tonic to minds disturbed; it was the philosophic defense of free will by Renouvier; it was the growing psychological belief on his own part that psychoses do not always depend upon neuroses and so may be got at directly—it was these artistic and scientific and philosophical medicines that cured him.

Morale recovered thus through empirical rather than magical means, his own perspective was left unblurred. He could genially conclude his own treatise on religious experience with the notion that "for each man to stay in his own experience, whate'er it be, and for others to tolerate him there, is surely best." He could inveigh against learned men who thought science a secure acquisition rather than a method of advance. He could hold overbeliefs himself, never failing to mark where evidence left off and hypothesis began. He could even demand for the underdog the right to have what experience he could have and to believe up to, rather than beyond, his lights. But he could not recommend to other men the religious way of life as long as there was anything else to recommend, and he could not himself practice it even then. "There was no sense of security," as Santayana with clearest discernment says of him, "no joy in James' apology for personal religion. He did not really believe; he merely believed in the right of believing that you might be right if you believed." When he saw the crowd of orthodox salvation-seekers he was drawing around him from men of little humor, he could but seek to puff them away with the sincere but stinging judgment that "what most religious men most need is that their faiths should be broken up and ventilated, that the northwest wind of science should get into them and blow their sickliness and barbarism away." Saved thus from religious morbidity, he was free to follow his speculative interests in discovering new vistas and blazing new paths for science, paths even into territory hitherto preserved as sacred.

I

Philosophy James took to be such a statement of the method and attitude of science as made it available for fulness of living. He not infrequently complains at the scientists; but it is because he feels that they have defined their method too narrowly or overestimated their finished achievement. He proposes no substitute for or supplement to science, only further application of it and humane tolerance meanwhile. Consequently we are not surprised to see him turn to construct a philosophy that is hardly more than a progressive generalization of the scientific attitude into the whole of life. His prejudices, as we shall see, were those of the scientific man. We do not need to emphasize how whole-heartedly James regarded philosophy as a way of living. The exposition of his position, to which we now turn, will be a continuous illustration of that thesis.

That philosophy can tell men *what* to believe James found to be an old and a common notion. Yet it is clear that men's beliefs should have something to do with facts. Human beings can never know all the facts in advance of crucial situations. Could they, the situations would, when they occur, be humdrum, not crucial. If philosophy is adequately to function as a way of life, it must emphasize the method of finding and harmonizing facts more than the fixing of attitudes in advance of occasions. Philosophy starts, James sees, as the articulation of one's own temperamental slant upon things. It may end there. Or it may become wider than one's own view through the discovery that there are others of like temperament whose outlooks can all receive a common statement. James was fond of dividing men into two temperamental groups—the tender-minded and the tough-minded. But if there is to be one philosophy rather than two or more, or if there is to be any way differentially to judge two or more, it is clear that a way of life must be found that can be hon-

estly recommended to both tough-minded
and tender-minded persons. What can
clearly be recommended to both is a method
of finding the facts and of getting what they
want. That is science. They may want different things, but clearly both must be able
to ascertain facts before either can get what
it wants. The relation of wants to philosophy we shall presently discuss, but now for
James' emphasis upon method. He was
early convinced that the only problem that
most men solve "is not one of being, but of
method."

James conceived philosophy to hinge
upon two closely related functions—a method of looking at problems and a theory of
the nature of truth. The former he illus-
trates simply with the story of the man who
goes round the tree in trying to discover a
squirrel that is also going round the tree
to keep from being discovered. The man
clearly goes round the tree on which the
squirrel is, but does he also go round the
squirrel? We may argue until doomsday
about it unless we agree to make a distinction. "Going round" the squirrel may legiti-
mately mean either going round where the

squirrel is or seeing in succession all sides of the squirrel. If we mean the former, then we can agree that the man goes round the squirrel; if we mean the latter, we must admit that he does not go round the squirrel. That is all there is to the problem. Meeting a difficulty, we have made a distinction; and with the distinction, the problem has disappeared. But what is the nature of the distinction that we have made and what the conclusion that we may draw from it? We have agreed to come down from abstract heights where going round means "just going round" in general and to settle ourselves consciously on a more concrete level where going round means something so specific that definition helps to clarify the situation and observation concludes the issue. The moral of this illustration is of universal import: ideas and theories are born of facts and have their sole fertility in relation to the facts.

James' emphasis upon the concrete borrows significance from historic contrasts. The weightiest tradition, though not the only one, in philosophy has supported the point of view we have seen developed by Royce. As between general notions and specific factual details, the historic preference has been for the former. Through the mouth of Socrates, Plato stated the case for abstractions beautifully. Socrates had heard that an older Greek philosopher taught that mind is the cause of all things. But when Socrates discovered what was meant by this, he was desperately disappointed; for what Anaxagoras meant was that some agency called mind pushed or pulled other elements in nature about. What Socrates had hoped to have established was that the real reason why anything is what it is, is that it is better for it to be that way than any other. He wanted not an explanation of the universe but an apology for it. Plato proceeded to give his successors what Socrates had sought in his predecessors. Taking such general notions as blueness, beauty, goodness to present one level of the universe and concrete blue things, beautiful objects, and good things another level, Plato explained the lower level in terms of the higher level rather than the higher in terms of the lower. Beauty is not just a simplified description of all the beautiful objects we know. To the contrary, objects are beautiful, according to him, because they have borrowed something from beauty itself.

Now it is clear, as we saw from Royce, that if one makes this approach he can by a proper selection of general principles not merely explain the good of experience but can also explain away the bad. If there is no generalized evil, then there can be no specific evils. James calls this apologetic attitude "tender-minded," because he thinks that such philosophers as Plato have had constitutions so weak that they were not able to take life straight; it must be diluted before they could drink it with impunity. Reminiscent of his own infirmity, James explained to his brother, Henry, why he took a scientific appointment at Harvard when he wished a philosophic one: "I am not a strong enough man to choose the other and nobler lot in life, but I can in a less penetrating way work out a philosophy in the midst of the other duties." Later, when he was strong again and had become a philosopher, he was to summarize his judgment of the tender-minded in one sentence, "Rationalism is comfortable only in the presence of abstractions."

Against this classic tradition, James opposed his own mature philosophy with the observation that "pragmatism is uncomfortable away from the facts." Philosophy, then, like science, must start with the facts. The universe was here before man came. Man cannot conjure it away by any process of reasoning; it remains to mock his neatest conclusion. Reasoning is important, tremendously important, but only in proportion as it starts from and ends with facts. No general notions have any validity or significance apart from the specific materials of experience to which they stand inexorably related. Freedom and security achieved through general notions are both specious unless buttressed by some better ordering of concrete experience. As method, then, philosophy looks from abstractions back to facts. Not concepts, but percepts are its hope. By its fruits, not by its roots, as James has it, are we to judge the tree of knowledge.

Adequately to see the justification, however, for this preference for the concrete, we must now consider James' philosophy as a theory of truth. James was not scientific merely in the sense of siding with the historic tradition that counted facts more important than theories, detailed experience more significant than general notions; but he was scientific also in the sense of building his philosophy upon the results of the modern evolutionary temper. Though from the first consideration he dedicates his *Pragmatism* to John Stuart Mill, "for whom," as he says, "I first learned the pragmatic openness of mind and whom my fancy likes to picture as our leader were he alive to-day," yet illustrating the second consideration the insight of Darwin is written large in James' thought.

As an evolutionist, James saw the human species as a newcomer upon an old scene. Pushed forward by his own vital impetus, man not infrequently stumbles over obstacles in nature which antedated his coming, or finds himself in conflict with his fellows for exclusive possession of limited goods, or even ensnarled in his own emotional complexity. Born to act and to feel, man's vocation is to act freely and to feel harmoniously. Among the biological variations that brought the human species to pass was the ideational process—the appearing in present experience of representatives of absent objects or experiences to guide endeavor to future satisfactions.

For ideas are just that. Illustrating both the lethargy and the prodigality of nature, ideas do not arise as long as action goes on satisfactorily and the emotional tone of life flows harmoniously. We live most of our waking life—and all of our sleeping life— much as the other animals; the completion of one action serves to initiate another, and one emotion gives birth to another without the aid of any midwife. But when our activity is blocked or our emotions get crisscrossed, ideas appear—appear not infrequently in profusion. Some are mere daydreams, some are irrelevant suggestions, some are mellow reminiscences, some are diverting distractions, but some are proposals to improve our position by action. Born of maladjustment, they serve—if serve they do—to improve adjustment of man to nature and to other men.

Here is evident the nucleus of what we have called the scientific way of life. Once ideas have appeared, they may be treated as objects in themselves and enjoyed or reprobated. So the aesthetic person treats them. They may be personified and deified and worshiped for their own majesty or for reward. So the religious person treats them. Or they may be regarded as having a history that suggests their function and a career that tests their value. It is the essence of the scientific attitude to regard them, like all things else, as functions of the past and as harbingers of the future. Since they purport to be guides to conduct, or programs of activity, they invite inspection on the basis of performance. The chief concern with them is whether they live up to promise.

James' theory of truth constitutes his specific treatment of this matter of ideas. The terms "true" and "false" apply only to ideas or beliefs. It is true that in a widely accommodated sense we sometimes apply them to other things, but never directly and literally. Arising to redirect action or to reenergize feeling, ideas are true that do so, false that do not. A man's promise is true if it turns out as indicated, false if it turns out otherwise. Drawing from James himself as convenient, let us illustrate this matter at its simplest. I am taking a walk in the forest adjoining my camp. If I am thinking at all, it is about other things than the walk or the camp, but suddenly I become aware of the fact that I have lost my bearings. Dinner time nears and I am hungry. Which is the way home? Several notions as to direction and paths arise in rapid succession. Shall I go this way or that or the other? Each is an idea of how to get back to camp. None is true in itself, but each is true or false with relation to the camp. Each is a plan of activity: what I am to do from here on. I cannot go more than one way at once. After deliberation, I make a choice between the idea-programs, either by flipping a coin or by other more cautious processes of elimination. This direction seems to me right, and that path looks promising. My idea or theory or notion or hypothesis (all these terms in philosophy meaning roughly the same thing) is that in this way I shall get back to camp. If I do get back to camp, my idea was a true one; if I do not, it was false.

James goes still farther than this. It is not merely that the satisfactory outworking of the idea shows it to be true, but also makes it to be true. Truth is not merely proved through, but is also constituted by, verification. Truth is not anything that an idea has as a birthright; it is something that happens to it in action. Activity is always necessary to constitute an idea true; for ideas arising in action are promissory of something to come from action. The outcome constitutes the promise true or false. It will be clearly seen that man is constantly regarded as a creature of evolution whose life depends upon continuous adjustment to a changing environment. Ideas are instruments for facilitating both active and passive adaptation. No adjustment is ever perfect, and even if it were, would not be final; for circumstances change and we ourselves grow. Out of maladjustment, therefore, ideas constantly arise to facilitate living. In one sense ideas always reflect the world we have known: they are copies of a past experience or experiences which, if we had them now combined thus or so, would be more satisfactory than what we do have. Ideas reflect the dual nature of our senses.

We have two kinds of access to our world through the senses. There is touch and taste that serve us only when we meet our world face to face: we taste only such things as get inside us and touch only such things as are at hand. But we have also eyes, ears, and a nose. The nose, to be sure, is a contact sense; but because of the volatile nature of much of our world it serves also as a distance sense. Our distance senses greatly enlarge our lives; they give us perspective; but we cannot live upon them. Not only can they not feed us, but they leave us subject to great errors. Never so sure are we of the nature of things as when we get them in our mouths or at least in our hands. Ideas have their forms from the distance senses, particularly from the eye. We see things with "the mind's eye" even farther away than with the other eye, but always in something of the same fashion. But just as the contact senses check up on the distance senses in our physical life, so also do all the senses check up on ideas in the life of mind. Ideas represent absent objects, but whether truly we can never tell until through our activity the absent objects are brought to us or we are transported to them. When we see things, we are more certain than when we think them; and when we feel them, we are more certain still. Thinking is clearly, then, a useful and far-reaching method of adjustment; but it is not final in itself, not self-validating. It derives from sensory experience and finds its certification in an enriched life of the senses. The intellectual pride which seeks to render thinking self-contained is as sterile as the reputed Chinese practice of living off each other's laundry.

The useful rôle that ideas and thinking play in overt action is indicative of their rôle in feeling. Emotion and action are, to be sure, very closely related; so closely related in James' philosophy, indeed, that emotion is always the report of muscular tonus. But if we consider them for the moment separately, ideas arise when our emotional life runs other than smoothly; they represent methods of adjustment; and they have here also their truth function in relation to outcome. And so with relation to emotion or action, "ideas (which themselves are but parts of our experience) become true just in so far as they help us to get into satisfactory relation with other parts of our experience." Since ideas, then, are exclusively instruments for a more prosperous adjustment, and since a man's philosophy is but the systematization of his ideas, philosophy comes squarely and solely to be a way of life whose objective is the freest action and the fullest emotions of which one is capable. A philosophy is true in so far as it is good, and it is good in so far as it maximizes living.

We see again, then, that what James has done is to take the method of science as it is applied in the laboratory to limited data and apply it to the whole of human thinking. Every idea is a hypothesis whose truth depends just as much upon its verification as does that of the most rigorous scientific construct. But thinking as a whole stands subordinated to man's emotional and practical needs, as in civilization science stands devoted to human ends. Intellectual pride leads to sterility, like intermarriage of royal families. Individual thinking is a form of action, as organized science is a form of social engineering. This subservience of thought to action and feeling led James to his best known, though perhaps most equivocal formulation, "The Will to Believe."

II

James' apparent betrayal of science in this famous essay grows out of one and only one consideration. He is as clear there as elsewhere that ideas and beliefs are by nature hypotheses, and so subject to the scientific demand for verification before they can be finally and fully trusted. He who can verify a belief and does not is flabby in his tendermindedness. To see that James believed this, one need only re-read the essay in question. To see that he practiced it, one need only note how cautiously after a quarter-century investigation of "psychical" phenomena James concludes that he needed "more facts before concluding." "At most," he again says of such phenomena, "they lead to the opinion that it may be well to keep a window open upon that quarter in one's mind." James is always and ever clear that "to pass from mystical to scientific speculations is like passing from lunacy to sanity." There is "no fatal lack in the spirit and principles of science"; such lack as exists grows out of the unwillingness of scientific men to believe enough in their method to apply it to all orders of facts. Much of life is left without the cleansing and guiding influence of science because of this narrowness of men of science. James intended in the name of science to correct the insensitivity and narrowness of professional men of science.

The field most neglected by science in James' day was, in his estimation, the human personality. James not only felt but also discerned this to be a center of things. "The only form of thing that we directly encounter, the only experience that we concretely have, is our own personal life." Here at least is the incidence of all things else upon us. The direction of social science in our time both acknowledges and pays a debt to James for this emphasis. While admitting the propriety of scientific interest in all fields and soliciting it wherever improvement awaits understanding—and where does it not?—James sees that meanwhile men must go on living. Man's emotional life profits most from tested and therefore completely dependable beliefs; but when these are not available, it can profit from beliefs only probable. And when even differential probability is lacking, some belief is still most likely to prevail. What belief is better for scientific testing and pending that, for plain human living, than one that represents the direction of our own emotional thrust? It is not merely a question of what should be, but also a question of what actually is. Do we or do we not tend to believe what we want to believe? Is man's emotional or his rational life primary?

When the previous question is thus raised, James does not hesitate to give the previous answer—we are creatures of action and impulse, and intelligence has its function in maximizing these. Indeed, rationality is, in his terminology, "a sentiment." Life is action, whatever our theory of it may be. The demands of action not infrequently if not always outrun scientific evidence. It adds to our uncertainty and risk that it is so; but if we take these to be bad, it is not the part of wisdom to increase them. To refuse to act or to act fearfully is definitely at times to increase our hazards. To act and to act confidently is at times to decrease our hazards. To believe in ourselves and in our universe, that is confidently to expect a prosperous outcome of what we admit to be a chance, this is to insure ourselves with whatever in-

surance is available in a precarious world.
This a good healthy human animal will do as
a matter of fact: and what a good healthy
animal does is what he should do, even
though in advance he cannot scientifically
prove that it will turn out well. If he knows
that not to act bodes ill and that to act with
confidence bodes less ill than not to act or
than to act without confidence, then indeed
the faith that converts a necessary equiv-
ocality into a maximum success has justified itself.

It is upon this right that James thinks
himself to insist in his doctrine of the will to
believe. The doctrine is a statement, first, of
what he regards a psychological fact, and,
second, of what he regards a moral theory.
Though the two are mixed, they are separable; and it is clear that when they are separated, the moral theory grows out of the psychological fact. James goes on the unargued,
though sound, premise that what men naturally and actually do is good and right, unless,
it turns out less satisfactory than something
else they might have as naturally and actually done. Morality is not a demand laid
forcibly upon experience; it is rather a choice

among the possibilities of experience in the light of their differential outcomes. "Our passional nature not only lawfully may, but must, decide an option between propositions, whenever it is a genuine option that cannot by its nature be decided on intellectual grounds." If James be right in his discernment of psychological fact, it is clear that he cannot be wrong in his moral advice, unless one hold the unlikely theory that ethics counsels what is impossible to practice.

Where James's argument was weak, and where it may be said to their credit that his critics got the better of him, is in his failing to emphasize throughout that what actually determines the right to believe is the antecedent probability of successful outcome. It is not a sheer right snatched out of the blue to follow as basic want some momentary whimsicality. What James really means to praise is the careful use of *whatever evidence there may be* that this alternative if believed will facilitate the outcome more than will that alternative. This is scientific so far forth. Certainly no scientific mind will despise evidence merely because it is meager, or will justify a person's acting against evidence because what he has is small. To use what evidence one has to make available as much more as is possible—this is the scientific attitude with regard to practical living. James has been severely criticized because it was thought that he was going against this principle. It must be admitted that James did lay himself open to suspicion here. His illustrations were clear enough—cases in which "faith in a fact could help create the fact." But his crucial objectives were not so clear. He permitted his doctrine to desensitize him to much relevant evidence as to how a belief works, and on narrowly individualistic foundations he allowed himself to ground theological faith.

It is not clear in the first place how acceptance of such beliefs as the existence of God can help make them into facts unless they are facts already; for such beliefs are *as to facts* rather than as to feelings or action. To be made happy by believing them does not prove it true when you would not have been happy with your belief had you not assumed it to be true. Whether such beliefs are facts or fictions is unknown, and must presumably remain unknown to the end of time. The only advantages therefore of believing them, disadvantages of not believing them, upon which we can rely to judge their moral worth are effects other than those that determine their factuality. They are such effects as the happiness of men who believe or disbelieve. Each side here claims the victory, and it is a pyrrhic victory as to the question at issue, whoever wins it. Since James saw that science is the only general method of verification for any beliefs that are verifiable, he was obligated to be sensitive to the effects of theological beliefs upon the prosperity of science, as well as upon the individual happiness of believers. It is the fact that he seemed willing to rest his judgments here upon individual rather than social good, upon short-run rather than long-run results, that in the last analysis subjects him not merely to moral suspicion but to logical inconsistency as well. Troubled by the unhappiness skepticism brought humble folk, he neglected its basic advantages in the progress of science through the centuries. He neglected it because, as he said, the individual man "plays the game of life for gains; and it is now or never with him, for the long run which exists

indeed for humanity, is not there for him."
(Is it not the business of educators and all
wise leaders *to make it there for him?*) This he
concludes immediately after admitting that
"the command laid upon us by science to believe nothing not yet verified by the senses is
a prudential rule intended to maximize our
right thinking and minimize our errors *in the
long run*. In the particular instance we must
frequently lose truth by obeying it: but on
the whole we are safer if we follow it con-
sistently, for we are sure to cover our losses
with our gains." That states the whole case
against James out of his own mouth, and
leaves completely triumphant in his domain
the scientific way of life.

It has already been indicated that James
himself was personally much more indifferent to such dogmas than his spirited defense
of the right to believe them would suggest.
He was himself so open-minded, in the best
scientific sense of the term, and so individualistic, in the ethical sense of the term, that he
could not bear to see scientific men deny
individuals the right to believe, even though
they denied it in the interest of the social
good. His scientific preference for particu-

lars became ultra-scientific when applied to individuals. There are other grounds for noting that he was relatively insensitive to social welfare when individuals stood between him and the light. "I am against bigness and greatness in all their forms, and with the invisible molecular moral forces that work from individual to individual . . . . against all big organizations; against all big successes and big results, and in favor of the eternal forces of truth which always work in the individual." James' bias in favor of religious persons and their right to believe whatever makes them feel better for the moment is reminiscent of his early soul-sickness, from which had he not recovered by natural means, he vaguely felt that he ought to have had the right to recover any way he could. Though he admits that it would not and should not convince others, he nevertheless submits as evidence for the legitimacy of psychical research his impression that two friends—Hodgson and Myers—grew "ever handsomer and strong-looking while engaged in it." "When a man's pursuit gradually makes his face shine and grow handsome, you may be sure it is a worthy one."

Practicing what he preached, James saw what he wanted to see. He does not seem seriously to have raised the question as to whether individuals are even in the short run better off from believing specious dogmas. He simply assumes, with the most superstitious people, that they are; and so he really does not come to grips with the scientists who on evidence assume the opposite. It may very well be that even in the short run of an individual's life, as James seems to admit for the longer run of the race, happiness is intensified through the caution recommended by Clifford, never to believe anything upon insufficient evidence. At any rate one rarely, if ever, meets a person who has achieved open-mindedness or even skepticism about doubtful matters who seriously shows himself willing to go back to the happy stage of credulity. James was certainly no candidate for such beatific reversion. But the obvious fact that James does not preoccupy himself with such questions serves to recall that he took little interest in any problems relating to social organization and educational control. He was individualistic in his prejudices as well as in his scientific theory. To say so but presents James again as a man for whom the individual is first and foremost, and as a thinker for whom philosophy never becomes a consistent body of doctrine objectively true but remains first and last a way of life adaptable to the temperamental needs of different individuals.

III

To complete the picture of James, we must comment upon his radical empiricism —a doctrine which he desired to have distinguished from his pragmatism. Whatever other purpose this doctrine served, it furnished James variety. In a pinch he did not think inconsistency too heavy a price for even a philosopher to pay for variety. Looked at in the large, radical empiricism was a view of nature which tended to relieve pragmatic truth of its excessive relativity and pragmatic living of temperamental audacity. The pragmatic view of truth made true whatever ideas worked well while they worked well for whom they worked well. And the insistence upon the primacy of the passional nature made valid so far forth any philosophy that made any man happy. Happiness, however, became through James' theory of emotions a corollary of muscular tonicity; and ideas through his doctrine of their genesis from inhibition became motor adjustment. Why not, then, simplify both thinking and feeling into physical relations between natural bodies? By his suggestion that consciousness does not exist James proceeded to translate into physical relations what had been regarded as escaping naturalism through attribution of "psychical." Human activity depends upon, is supported by, and sometimes modifies the natural order. In dissipating consciousness into objective relations, James diminishes the relativity of truth by making ideas relative to a set of *abiding* relations in the natural world. Moreover, for a man hereafter to follow his temperament is but to adapt himself to what is utterly different from whim, to a natural order scientifically conceived. The mind empties itself of all ideas and feelings, and feels great relief, for a time. As Santayana says, "To deny consciousness is to deny a prerequisite to the obvious, and to leave the obvious standing alone. That is a relief to an over-

taxed and self-impeded generation: it seems
a blessed simplification. It gets rid of the
undemocratic notion that by being very re-
flective, circumspect and subtle you might
discover something that most people do not
see. The elimination of consciousness not
only restores the obvious, but proves all
parts of the obvious to be equally real . . . .
All fictions and all abstractions are now declared to be parcels of the objective world;
it will suffice to live on, to live forward, in
order to see everything as it really is."

But it is foregone that the relief thus
achieved would not be permanent. When
tired of an order with its relations ready-
made, James swung back to a more loose-
jointed world where he could make relations
at will. Against the idealists, it was good
argument to point out that the world hung
together by its own relations. But when the
new realists ran away with this world all
naturally geared up and then quite logically
pointed out that even the human mind had
no function save to discover and to behold
pre-existing relations, James was uneasy at
finding his marvelous personal energy super-
annuated. As his psychological voluntarism

emptied into behaviorism and his logical empiricism emptied into realism, he oftentimes felt sympathetic toward some notion of universal spirit(s). Thus did he drop fertile spores into many fields from his never empty Pandora box.

Whenever and in so far as James got away from the scientific postulate of the uniformity and continuity of nature, he tended to repair the hazards of discontinuity by postulating a deity whose aid, even if finite, would strengthen human hope of triumph in an otherwise unpredictable universe. When his universe grew in mellow moods of audacity into a pluriverse and threatened to burst with sheer variety, he tended strongly to believe in panpsychism, whereby the diverse elements would still hold together by will if not by constitution.

For purposes of practice, his eventuations seemed always to possess standard characteristics. The world of his heart's desire must have variety without wholly lacking security. Scientific uniformity to the point of mechanism—a point to which, as he saw, it strongly tended—gave security through predictability, but left no fun and adventure in life. Loosen up the mechanistic notion so as to allow variety, and you may lose the assurance of a happy outcome. Not, however, if you can in the process of loosening discover in the cosmic crevices a superhuman energy to support you and to elicit your support through loyalty. How strongly this idea of a finite God may be made to appeal both to one's sense of loyalty and to aspiration for improvement, one cannot but see in the closing chapter of James' *Pragmatism* or, on another level, in H. G. Wells' *God the Invisible King*. If, however, the liberty-adventure motif gets too much for man and his finite God, then gravitate toward idealism and conceive the universe itself in its own right to be spiritual. If this pass tends to run one back into as suffocating a spiritual oneness as does science into a materialistic monism, then make the spiritual order pluralistic and keep variety without sacrificing insurance of desired eventuation. James indeed called his empiricism "radical" because it insisted upon treating monism itself as an hypothesis rather than as a fact.

IV

Through all his changes James himself lived adventurously with none too much worry over consistency. He could not accept a rigid naturalism, such as his realistic disciples were developing at the time of his death; for he never gave up the hypothesis that immortality might be a fact. He never believed in it "keenly," as he said, "but more strongly as I grow older; because I am just getting fit to live." He could not accept a rigid theism, on the other side. He wrote to a friend that his system was "theistic, but not *essentially* so." He accepted, more or less opportunistically, what seemed necessary to him at given stages, and hoped that if his various beliefs were too inconsistent, it was because the universe itself was discontinuous and pluralistic. But it must not, in turn, grow so pluralistic as to invalidate optimism of a fruitful outcome of our human venture. Among the general lessons that James has to teach us stands most prominent this: To take the philosophic way of life does not necessarily mean to commit oneself to a single system or to an inflexible idea of consistency. The philosopher can always find reasons for believing whatever he believes.

And yet it is but fair to say in concluding the sketch of this many-sided man that his "overbeliefs"—as he called what clearly went beyond scientific criteria—were believed "north northwest." Perhaps never before did a man hold in such genuinely hypothetical fashion such traditional and emotion-laden beliefs. Immortality was a conjecture; the existence of God a hypothesis; psychical contact with a spiritual realm a possibility. His mind remained as open after twenty-five years of psychical research as at the beginning. Himself with no genuine mystic experience of any sort, though in early life pitiably subjected through grave soul-sickness to the worst sort, he held out nevertheless for an open mind on the part of those who took upon themselves the great name of science. He disclaimed against nothing scientific save the intolerance of scientific men. In this he was more scientific than they. He spoke never against scientific method. He generalized scientific technique, indeed, into a philosophy of life. He confronted scientific complacency with new worlds to conquer through bold application of its own method. He did so because of this insistent and wise question that often came to him: "When was not the science of the future stirred to its conquering activities by the little rebellious exceptions to the science of the present?" Though sympathetic with those who in ignorance or under pain slipped an intellectual cog now and then, he himself knew as few men have known what has been proved, what constitutes proof, and what is merely hypothesis. He exemplified the scientific attitude over a very wide field; and he lived it out to the last, leaving these words for his friends when they could have him no longer: "There is no conclusion. What has concluded that we might conclude in regard to it? . . . . Farewell."

With a hearty farewell to James, we shall now journey with a guide who without emphasizing science less, emphasizes its social setting more.

CHAPTER IV

THE SOCIAL WAY OF LIFE WITH JOHN DEWEY AS GUIDE

Words soon are cold, and life is warm for ever.
One half of honour is the strong endeavour,
Success the other, but when both conspire
Youth has her perfect crown, and age her old desire.
— SANTAYANA

SOME philosophers look at life and see beauty; some look at life and see nature; some look at life and see themselves; some look at life and see other men. John Dewey is of the latter type. He sees men wherever he looks. Nor does he see merely the leaders of men; he sees men themselves. He fain would set all intelligence to work for human good. Scanning the sea of life, he discerns no ship save humanity.

. . . . vast outbound ship of souls,
What harbor town for thee?
What shapes, when thy arriving tolls,
Shall crowd the banks to see?
Shall all the happy shipmates then
Stand singing brotherly?

> Or shall a haggard ruthless few
> Warp her over and bring her to,
> While the many broken souls of men
> Fester down in the slaver's pen,
> And nothing to say or do?

His deepest and most insistent note is that of community. Men stand so immovably in the center of his vision that he sees nothing save through them—nature herself gets humanized or remains outside the picture. His philosophy is, of course, the story of what he sees. "Philosophy," he has said, "recovers itself when it ceases to be a device for dealing with the problems of philosophers and becomes a method, cultivated by philosophers, for dealing with the problems of men." How this social focus stands related to life and to nature as its fringe we shall see by looking at various aspects of the total scene through the eyes of this genuine humanist.

I

We are invited to see thinking itself through his eyes. Thinking is not, we at once discover, abstract relations laid out in nature, as some philosophers have thought; nor is it something back of nature that caused and sustains nature, as others have believed; nor is it yet a human activity whereby we discern what is in or back of nature, as still others have taught. Thinking is the most efficient method yet discovered for nature to carry on through us her evolutionary career. Genuine parts of nature ourselves, we partake of her life; we are her most flexible instruments of variation; she saves, as it were, many a step for herself by staging through us dramatic rehearsals of possibilities before committing herself to actualize them. Looking on at this show, we applaud the plays we like; and, behold, the stage disappears and we note that our approval has made the stage life and the characters real; or we sit impassive before a rehearsal; and, behold, we wake to find that it was a dream. Nature thinks through us, but it is our profit as well as her career. So greatly, indeed, do we profit from the performance that we call it our doings, and set ourselves the task of improving an instrument so potent.

We analyze this fertile activity, and find that it falls into separable aspects. It arises, as James also saw, from inhibited activity.

To clarify the hindrance is to facilitate the process of thinking. From the clarification, suggestions arise as to how to resume the interrupted activity. Past experience comes to our aid, and each suggestion proliferates into a train of acts that as it unrolls solicits our approval or disapproval. We find ourselves passing without break from the dramatic rehearsal of possibilities to overt acts after the pattern of the one that intrigues us most. The fruits in action are as sweet as they seemed to imagination and our thought has succeeded, or something was not foreseen and action reveals our error only to set us to work anew upon another tack. Endlessly thus do we pass from imagination to action, correcting the one by the other, and enriching the other by the one. Such adjustment of ourselves to our environment through the provocation it offers and the reconstruction in it we effect constitutes the career of thinking. It is man participating in nature, recreating nature, and creating himself as he participates. His past experience determines the fruitfulness of his suggestions in difficulties; his knowledge of what are called natural laws determines his ability to rehearse possibilities before action; and his emotional generosity determines his ability to pick out for actualization those rehearsed possibilities which as they materialize will be luscious fruit rather than dead ashes.

But it will be clearly sensed that this process is not merely something that goes on in one's head. It involves both us and nature: its occasion lies deeper than thought, its eventuation is in nature rather than in man, and through it nature gets changed and man gets satisfied. Nor does it typify the relation between a mind and a finished reality. In a finished world there would be no occasion for thinking. In a wholly inchoate world there would be no possibility of consummated thinking. But in the kind of world this is, thinking does go on. So it must be a world where initiation really starts something and where eventuation finishes something satisfactorily. Since thought arises at the crossroads of activity and inactivity, and consists in confronting the unsatisfactory actual with an inviting possibility, thinking may be regarded as a process whereby the real is budged, be it however little, toward the ideal. To think is to facilitate natural evolution and to appropriate its fruits as interest for our part in the performance. But, like America's present international predicament, we know that whether we think or not, we shall get implicated in the affair. Evolution goes on with or without us. Thinking is our only way of participating in the process with a sound hope of differential gain.

II

We are invited to look at value through the eyes of this philosopher. Value cannot for one who, like Dewey, keeps man at the center of his thought be regarded as something that exists independently of man. It must, on the contrary, be the name of something that men actually experience. Once thus empirically placed, there is no good reason for not taking the perfectly commonsense view that value is whatever men prize, hold dear, desire. It is not something to be argued about by philosophers. Any abstract argument about what it is can be settled by asking whoever is concerned for a list of what he likes. But what is it apart from a given person? It is what any other abstraction is—an abstraction; and abstractions are not cases of value unless someone finds them to be valuable. Then their value is whatever anyone finds in them to prize. But if it be felt that this represents value on too low a scale—the scale of appetites and passions— Dewey replies that it is the presence of these that alone makes value possible and the satisfaction of these that alone makes value actual. But has thinking nothing to do with values?

Thinking does not initially create values. It is not needed to discover values. But it has a rôle to play in reconstructing and in perpetuating values. This rôle becomes clear when we apprehend Dewey's belief that experience is a much wider term than thinking. Thinking is only one form of experience, and it is a form that gets all its relevance and significance from another form of experience. This other form is that of feeling and doing. What goes on easily for us feels good, and what feels good is good. But what feels good at a given time may cease to feel good at another. It is, as we have already observed, when action lags or feeling sags toward pain that thinking arises. Thinking is a secondary, a derivative, form of experience that

serves as an instrument of evolution to maximize satisfaction. Dewey's theory of value
can be further clarified, if we detail the relation between this primary feeling-experience
and the foregoing instrumental thinking-
experience.

1. *Experience, which furnishes the context
of all values, is largely non-intellectual.*—It is
well to emphasize this non-thought basis of
thinking itself; for upon this plane of experi-
encing lies most of the content of our living.
Here are included our loves and hates, our
eating and our sleeping, our friendships and
our animosities, our illness and our health;
here too are the fine arts; here the dumb
gladness that welcomes the dawn, the quiet
contemplation of the sun's trailing glory at
eventide, and the silent watching of the
passing night. This is the primal and ever
the larger aspect of human life. It is the
good-in-itself, from which reflection arises
and for the sake of which reflection exists
as an instrument.

2. *Experience becomes thinking only when
incompatibilities demand more than mere appreciation for their successful resolution.*—
Dewey is primarily interested in intrinsic

values, the elemental experiences described in the foregoing. Indeed, no living being, thinks he, ever becomes interested in extrinsic values until he must in order to save and extend some of the immediate content of his appreciative life. Then thinking comes into play as an instrument that is justified by resolving the difficulty back into a situation that permits the immediate goods again to become possible. If thought begins, as with Royce, to build upon itself a hierarchy that forbids the energy of life to dip again into its stream, it meets Nemesis upon its upward way, who robs it of its vaunted glory and leaves it quite inane.

3. *Such adjustment arises from, exists for the sake of, and dips again into, unthinking experience.*—The vine of pedant theory, as Dewey has recently suggested, is attached at both ends to the pillars of felt values. Thinking becomes thus an instrument, but an indispensable instrument, for the continuous preservation and deepening of the values for which it exists.

4. *Moral judgments do not discover value outside experience, but reconstruct experience so as to make it more valuable.*—Let it be

carefully borne in mind what has been said about the genesis of thinking as such. Moral thinking differs from other types in no other way than to have as content experienced goods. Value judgments arise out of a situation made embarrassing by a conflict between two equally valuable parts of experience or out of some other equally unsatisfactory turn of experience; and the judgments are but citations of what seems necessary to make experience once more satisfactory. They are discoveries of what under the circumstances one ought to do, if he is successfully to resolve the unsatisfactory situation. The judging process is not only the discovering of what is to be done, but it is also the first step of the action itself. It is not a discovery of something already existent, because the situation to which the judgment looks as an end that is to resolve the maladjustment has never yet existed and would not come to exist but for the process of action which is initiated by the judgment itself. The restored equilibrium is the creation of the active life through thought as its tool. For an ill person to decide that it is well for him to see a doctor is but for him to take the

first step in the creation of the good of his
then situation, i.e., relief from his illness, a
good that but for his judgment would never
come to be at all.

While others have cried, "Lo, here; lo,
there!" Dewey has continually insisted that
the kingdom of good is within human experience. And this is all that Dewey is really
saying in his theory of value: values are immanent in human experience. They are
whatever men actually do prize. Take them
for what they are: if they are many, so
much the better; if they are found within
classes that aforetime were vulgar, judge the
classes by the values, rather than the values
by the classes. When Dewey insists that
values are *here*, he also indicates the very important social doctrine that they are *everywhere* here. No class has a monopoly upon
them; if so, the chief task of man is to see
that monopoly ended. To make values common to all men, to deepen them, and to
guarantee them—this is the threefold problem common to philosophy, to science, to
government. This is the problem of man.
The first step in the solution of the problem
is the whole-hearted recognition that values

are immanent in human experience, rather than secluded in some transcendental or conceptual realm accessible to common men only through priestly or philosophic or governmental intermediaries.

III

We are thus led to look at education through this philosopher's eyes. It will be seen in the first place that since change goes on continually and thinking is our way of participating in its fruits, education must be continuous if it has to do with thinking. The truth is, according to Dewey, that historically education has not been concerned primarily with thinking. It has been an instrument to prevent thinking. Thinking breaks new ground. The breaking of new ground endangers old structures. Institutions that get firmly established, classes that get strategically placed, unite in agreeing to minimize change and in monopolizing the fruits of what goes on irrevocably. Education easily becomes under such circumstances an indoctrination of each generation to respect the order which they find pre-existent. To induct one into the culture created for him, to generate in him respect for it and for its agents, to reconcile him to his lot in life, and to foreswear him to loyalty for the rights of others, as pre-established as his own lot— this is the story of traditional education. To keep the young out of mischief until they are old enough to go to work, this is education. If education has sufficiently engendered loyalty to the established order, law and government may be able to keep men at work for the profit of whoever profits by the status quo. Whoever gets the profits will be entitled to them, for he enforces the laws and superintends the education. It is just that he do this, for justice will have been defined as each one's doing his own work and each one's getting and keeping what belongs to him.

Once popular unrest makes inroads, however, upon a class system and democratic institutions arise as methods of equalizing opportunity, education acquires new objectives and gropes for new techniques. It then appears that a monopolizing of goods by one class is a work of presumption rather than of justice. Virtues as educational tools for justifying economic prerogatives must be democratized. To equalize educational opportunities themselves becomes the first step to all other changes. But to equalize a basic means implies equalization of ends to which the means points. The historic attempt to distribute luxuries to the commoners revealed even to commoners themselves that one reason that goods had been reserved for the few was that there were not enough for all. But it was early suspected also that the restriction of goods to the few was a reason why there were not enough for all. Once men had a right to them and had tasted hitherto reserved delights, they were ready to work to produce goods in larger quantities. How to produce enough to go round follows as a fruitful problem upon the acquisition of the right to pass them round. And education acquires a new function: how to make men more efficient producers.

The study of how to produce more goods not only leads to more goods but to different men. To invent and to manipulate machinery awakens new powers. It gives one, on a scale however small, a magic touch of control, and this breeds new respect for self and a sense of power that seeks further control and a sense of dignity that wishes not merely to have goods but also to be somebody. Moreover, study with others under equalizing conditions or work with others for results that are to be shared discovers to one social aptitudes in himself and unsuspected abilities and attractions in others. Social feelings and capabilities arise out of democratic education, and the making of goods, once the means are achieved and secured, seems less important than the making of men. Nor can the lesson learned in initiating technologies be forgotten: whatever men make, they remake themselves in the process. Everything is seen to be educational if it be carried on under favorable conditions— work for an adult no less than play for a child, and neither of these less than study in the school. The educational prerequisite is the same in each: conditions must be such that one may be brought face to face with the difficulties as they arise; must be enabled to regard them as his difficulties by having a stake in the results that come from a solution; must be able to pool with those of others his ideas as to the best solution; and must suffer his share from failures as well as profit from successes.

This is to say that education becomes a life process of growth with two major objectives: first, to facilitate and utilize all fruitful ideas as methods of natural control: and, second, to develop a co-operative spirit as the normal attitude in work and play. The first objective recognizes that thinking is the only human activity that minimizes the disadvantages and maximizes the advantages for man of the changes that an evolutionary philosophy assumes to be inevitable. It applies the doctrine that thinking arises from problematic situations, and it exemplifies the democratic faith that all men possess in ideational ingenuity what no men can afford to have go to waste. All men have scientific abilities, and all the abilities put together are no more than are needed to maintain at its best the human enterprise in the face of cosmic odds. The second objective recognizes that without a social spirit opportunities will not be sufficiently equalized to elicit continuously the full abilities of men. Moreover, it reveals one of the most profound discoveries that man has yet made, and that is that no amount of other goods can sufficiently compensate man for lack of sympathetic intercourse with his kind. Partnership, comradeship, friendship—these are the noblest ships in which to embark for the voyage called life. The modern democratic experiment, halting as it has been and as disappointing in results, has demonstrated as possible what all aristocrats have declared impossible—co-operation of common men in huge enterprises. The co-operation itself has not been perfect, but behold what it has already achieved! Starting out as separated individuals with inalienable rights all each one's own to get what belonged to them, common men have in less than two hundred years so learned the art of co-operation as not merely through factory production to fill the world with goods but through labor organizations to bid portentously, if not always effectively, for a growing share of both goods and industrial control. Seeing what has been achieved against great odds, reckless indeed would be the prophet who thinks the end of democracy has yet come. Like the phoenix, democratic aspiration rises to new life from every death. The co-opera-

tion necessary to achieve every democratic
end renders it far less selfish in realization
than it was in contemplation. Co-operation
breeds fellowship, and fellowship works for a
world in which men will not only have
friends but will be friends. In such a world
men could drop so many of their defenses
that they would stand revealed to one another as the supreme objects of desire and
enjoyment.

This is suggestive of sentimentalism, because heretofore its articulation has been
left largely to religious prophets and to
poets. In Dewey, however, the insight has
achieved a secular and philosophic spokes-
man, who reflects a background neither
pious nor sentimental. It is well for us to
explore that background.

IV

The key notion of Dewey's philosophy is
"shared experience." His psychology is devoted to showing that shared experience is
possible and how, and his ethics is devoted
to portraying its beauty and reward. We
shall here discover the deepest essence of
Dewey's way of life. The tradition that lies

back of modern democracy is one that all
but makes impossible the realization of democracy as fraternity; it is the egoistic not
to say downright selfish conception of
human nature. The individualism which
flowered into modern democracy postulates
that men naturally seek each his own good.
Government is explained as the result of the
conviction that men could get more out of it
than they put into it; it arose from a contract in which there was a generous *quid pro
quo*. Since government arose thus, the pattern is set for all legal transactions there-
under. Contract is the established social
bond in modern democracy; and contract is
conceived as a meeting of equal and independent minds for a consideration. The practical identity of contract and sociality has
permeated our whole modern life until marriage has become a contract and religion itself a covenant. Success means to retain
one's own independence and to get the best
of the other fellow; this must be so where
goods are limited and personality is conceived as disjunctive. Adam Smith postu-
lated an "invisible hand" to protect social
welfare; and, faith, it was needed when all

parties went to the bargain to get all they
could for themselves. The hand was, however, as impotent as it was invisible, if one
may judge by the rapacity of competition
throughout the first century of capitalism.
In practice, however, competition has in no-
table cases given way to co-operation, and
contract has ceased in fact to be the only
social relation. But the backwardness of our
theory of social relations has retarded our
advance in practice.

What has chiefly hindered the advance of
theory is the absence of a fundamentally different interpretation of human nature itself.
If men are created separate atoms in a social
void, doomed each to be self-seeking, then is
contract sanctioned by coercion the only dependable bond. But if the very notion of
contract implies a wider pre-existing social
milieu, then it may be that individuality is
an inclusive rather than exclusive thing. It
has been the spirited assertion of the latter
point of view that has characterized Dewey's
social psychology. So long, however, as the
old assertion that men are by nature bad was
confronted by nothing more than the coun-
terassertion that men are good, the counter-

assertion was hardly more convincing than the assertion. What was needed to raise human opinion of human nature to the actual level of human practice was a radical reinterpretation of the constitution of mind and individuality. This interpretation must needs take the form of a new genesis for human nature. Unsubjected to radical criticism, the notion of mind had been taken over from that of soul; and soul had a theological background in the shadows of which the devil had been all too active.

Dewey has been in the forefront of modern psychologists and sociologists who have been elaborating a different genealogy for the human soul. What is demanded for democratic purposes is that the soul should have a sociological rather than a theological pedigree. That nurture is highly important in the formation of character has always been seen. But character was for long supposed to be grafted onto a theological core. It remained for Darwin's insight to be applied to man and thus disclose the fact that men are sheer animals but for what they can elicit from one another through fruitful intercourse. Consider many of the animals:

they neither make contracts nor hand down judicial decision, and yet they sometimes go about in groups and seem quite well disposed toward one another. Evolution gives men a social ancestry. But more than this was needed as foundation for a social way of life. A mechanism is needed whereby a baby animal can ingrow a group pattern and thus become a man. Dewey and his disciples have by clarifying and emphasizing this mechanism been able to explain the fact of man's intrinsic sociability.

In the first chapter we have suggested speech as the major technique whereby creatures who start as animals end their careers as men. We need not here elaborate that suggestion. Born into a friendly group with a nurturing tradition older than the human species, man needs only a mechanism for appropriating the group pattern to make antecedently probable—may we not say certain?—his actual appropriation of it. So long as it was supposed that men came directly from God, it was accepted as reasonable that, in a pinch at least, they would find their chief function in glorifying God and enjoying him if possible. So long as it was affirmed that men came from the devil, or associated with him too intimately on their way from deity, it was regarded as certain that they would work for the devil. So also is it now foregone that if human nature is group-engendered, human conduct will tend to exemplify the social pattern. Since the outward has become the inward, the inward will in practice out again.

The chief problem for practice is to see that this comes about in a fruitful manner. This sociological derivation of personality does not mean, of course, that the knowledge of their evolution will convert men overnight from capitalists into saints. Indeed we should perhaps be the worse off for such a conversion: for capitalists supply capital, whereas saints supply only saintliness. But it does lay the basis in a more or less controllable environment for a hopeful approach to the social problem. It does clarify in theory what we have wondered about in practice, the intermixture of social motives with the most selfish practices. Indeed, it makes clear to us that there is no pure selfishness. Men steal that they may share with others what without stealing they cannot even them-

selves enjoy. Selfishness is never pure egoism, but at worst small group-ism. Indeed,
the whole line of thought makes possible for
the first time a continuity of understanding
between egoism and altruism, between selfishness and unselfishness.

The first light that appears is the discovery that the means of continuity between
the bad and the good is man himself. Selfishness and unselfishness are both alike functions of the "self." The moral crux is, therefore, not the presence nor the centrality of
the self in conduct, but the *kind* of self which
conduct expresses and promotes. A generous
self is one that promotes the welfare of the
"gens," or group; an ungenerous person is
one who serves less than the "gens." It is
not a moral injunction, but a psychological
fact, that no man liveth unto himself.

The second light is the discovery that
since the individual personality reproduces
the group in miniature, the only effective
way of individual betterment is social improvement. We have said oftentimes that
the only way to reform society is by increasing the proportion of good men. And in
a sense that is true no doubt. Far more sig-

nificant, however, is the converse statement. Most of the reforming of human character goes on in the forming of it.

Here, then, is implicit a norm that begins with the family and does not end this side of the state—a norm that would regulate the major human business of soul-growing. It perhaps has its clearest application in education, because the school has become in practice the corrector of personality disorders engendered in the family as well as the creator of personality defenses against the sovereign state. In so far as the family seeks to inculcate loyalty to itself as a group—and whatever impetus toward ideals remains in it is largely of this traditional sort—it conditions the emotions and sentiments of children to a progressively non-functioning nucleus, a conditioning that must certainly be unlearned before an objectively fruitful or a subjectively peaceful character can be developed. Not only must the emotional object be changed, but also the emotional bias. It is too much to expect a high order of success when the school meets this impediment; but the success of the school in building a good character will, nevertheless, depend largely upon its success in unconditioning the pride and narrowness and stunted curiosity evoked by family influence. The final appeal of the state, on the other hand, has been to patriotism, meaning the large-scale contradiction of all the piecemeal instruction the school gives the child in ideals: for patriotism still largely means that the child will eventually *kill*, will kill *intentionally*, will kill *for reasons unquestioned and even unknown*, and will *do it all gladly*. As James Russell Lowell puts it in his apostrophe to America:

> What were our lives without thee?
> What all our lives to save thee?
> We reck not what we gave thee,
> We will not dare to doubt thee,
> But ask whatever else and we will dare.

To expect thoroughgoing character conversion in adult life of a man who comes from a typical family and journeys toward a patriotic grave for a typical state is in all truth to expect a miracle. There is no hope from the cataclysmic approach to the problem of character development. It marks, according to Dewey, the chief remaining superstition of educated men. Though there is no hope here, there is much hope nevertheless. Men do have small loyalties, and they are capable of larger loyalties without limit. We know that men will live for parasitic families, and we know that men will die for despotic states. Between Scylla and Charybdis lie peaceful waters. Just societies will easily produce just men; but just men cannot produce just societies unless they regulate all the agencies of education and all the subtler organs of public opinion. There are, however, no absolutes to deter our daily best. "The bad man," as Dewey has it, "is the man who, no matter how good he has been, is beginning to deteriorate, to grow less good. The good man is the man who, no matter how morally unworthy he *has* been, is moving to become better." With a social foundation to character assured, nothing stands in the way of progressive socialization of society except lack of fruitful technologies backed by robust and undaunted wills. Even the cosmos itself Dewey seems to ally for social support.

V

What the nature of this support is and how far it reaches make a worthy concluding theme. Dewey has never been able, with such a thinker as Bertrand Russell, to regard man as a waif in the universe, shut out in the first place from assured knowledge of the world in which he lives and shut out in the second place from cosmic support for his aspirations. Whether Dewey's confidence in the universe draws more support from the Hegelian philosophy from which he came than from the naturalism he has himself developed, we may judge for ourselves. The universe is friendly, first, because we do actually know it. Men do not know ideas, but they know things through ideas; not through them in the sense that one sees a green world through a green glass, but through them in the sense that a traveler comes to know a country through the use of a map. Ideas are stimuli to action because they are suggestions of something more desirable through action than confronts one without action. If the suggestions they constitute are certified after and through action, the ideas are true and the certification is knowledge. Knowledge of what? Knowledge of nature herself both as she is and as she becomes through our action. But we ourselves are children of nature through an evolutionary pedigree. We are children, not orphans. We share her life, we carry on her work, we know her in knowing ourselves. Our experience has her very framework as its content. We no more experience "experience" than we have ideas of "ideas." Our ideas are of courses of action in relation to things, and our experiences are of things themselves. There is here such an "at-homeness" as makes it possible for Dewey to feel as well as to think that nature experiences herself through us.

Not all our thoughts need have counterparts in nature, however; nor need all that is in nature ever be in our thoughts. That there are possible experiences that have not yet been, and may never be, is certain. That there are things never yet known may be taken for granted; for science which finally certifies to us most indubitably that some of our experiences are of nature herself, lives the life of the expectant. Our experience is all that we shall ever know of the universe; and it is enough for us to know that nature is so far forth what she is experienced by us to be. Nature is friendly in that she has produced us as we are and reveals herself to us through our experience. Philosophy becomes the whole-hearted appreciation of all that experience reveals to be true or beautiful or good. She accepts also gratefully the negative safeguards of experience that science offers and just as gratefully the positive additions of meanings that come through art and morality. Nature is for us what she is continuously experienced by us to be.

It is this emphasis upon experience as philosophic method and as the measure of our metaphysical reach that constitutes Dewey's way of life finally and fully social. The only nature that concerns him is the nature of human experience. In Dewey's earlier idealism where experience was interpreted more intellectually, the experience of knowing not only encompassed the whole of nature but constituted nature as well. The later orienting of intellect in feeling and action does not prove that even the wider experience is as wide as the universe. Experience is no magic word. It is indeed at any given time a highly limiting word. Our experience, all told, encompasses only that part of the universe that it does encompass. Even though, according to Dewey, experience is not something inside living forms, it nevertheless cannot happen apart from them, and its realm is therefore limited to their reach. Now in all truth we as the highest organic forms do not reach very far—not very far into the past, not very far into the future, not very far into the vitals of the present. Actual human experience at any given time constitutes in fact so tiny a part of what we believe nature actually to be that one wonders at a philosopher's not being impressed by the discrepancy. Truly the rational is real, but the real is not thereby exhausted by the rational. Is Dewey's lack of interest in this fact explained by his division of the field with natural science or by the survival in emotion of an earlier intellectual belief that not only is the rational real but also that the real is the rational? However this be, the only nature that concerns Dewey is the one of experience, a humanistic nature rather than a metaphysical one.

But even the humanistic world indicates clearly enough that while this philosophy enables us to feel at home, it does not guarantee us a home. For the nature experienced by us is full of clashing powers. Not even the part known as ourselves ever achieves complete integration. If nature is throughout what our limited experience of inner disharmony and outer stress reveals, she is cold and indifferent as well as warm and pulsing, whimsical and arbitrary as well as docile and touched with reason. The precarious, as Dewey shows, is at least as basic a trait in her as is the stable. Our longing for the stable is not in itself to be taken as indicative that nature actually is more stable than she seems or that she can by our efforts be eventually made as stable as we wish. In spite of its humanism, there is here no satisfactory philosophy for one who demands as part of his way of life some guaranty of continued personal or racial fulfilment. It may as well be as otherwise that nature co-operates with us as we co-operate with the animals whom we fatten for food. Nature perhaps yearns to us because, to adapt Hardy's lines,

> . . . . When we surcease
> Through whom alone lives she,
> Her spirit ends its living lease,
> Never again to be!

The motif, then, that in other philosophies has created gods and guaranteed immortalities here gets no farther than to counsel a spirit of participation in the on-going universe—going on for aught we know, for most that moderns suspect, to our eventual doom. Our day is ours; let us improve it. Thinking is our instrument, education is our means, democratic government is our safeguard. We can find our own significance, and some solace for our woes, in the limited future of our race. Since we do participate in nature; since our thinking not only reveals her but at times reconstructs her, we can through humane conduct increase our own joy and through co-operative control make her more habitable for our children. It is the feel of this omnipresent social bond and the challenge of a finer race yet to be that takes the place—if take it, it can—of older theodicies and newer theologies. A genuine partnership with nature, an affinity with humanity that has produced us and a humanity that we may ourselves help produce, a lack of preoccupation over one's own personal fate— these constitute the major guideposts in the Deweyan way of life.

CHAPTER V

THE AESTHETIC WAY OF LIFE
WITH GEORGE SANTAYANA
AS GUIDE

The muffled syllables that Nature speaks
Fill us with deeper longing for her word;
She hides a meaning that the spirit seeks,
She makes a sweeter music than is heard.
—Santayana

AS WE turn to George Santayana for the last illustration of idea-ways of life, we meet a genial mentor. As he hands us his latest philosophy, he matches our smile with a twinkle. I am merely attempting to express for you, he gestures deprecatingly, the principle to which you appeal when you smile. "For good or ill, I am an ignorant man, almost a poet, and I can only spread a feast of what everybody knows." Here is geniality that disarms resistance and insinuates itself antecedent to criticism. It inspires confidence as do the self-depreciations of a hardened guide who whimsically understates his knowledge of paths and woods, of streams and game. Santayana leads us to expect much from life because he promises so little, and yet promises it so good-naturedly. From him we certainly should suffer no disappointment, save such as comes from accepting what we were from the first cautioned to avoid.

If we were obliged at the end to take Santayana as a guide to life at his own easy evaluation rather than at the higher one his modesty tempts us to make of him upon first acquaintance, we should nevertheless treasure him in memory. Wherever our jaunt with him may end, we shall certainly never have lovelier scenery than on this trip. If we find ourselves riding in our guide's own vehicles, it is our tribute to excellence. After Plato, Santayana is one of the few philosophers whom no living man may hope to improve by paraphrase. So lovely indeed are the literary flora and fauna of Santayana's native province—and he is native to much— that not a few have preferred to remain lost and wandering with him than to be rescued by others.

Though he whimsically deprecates his service, Santayana seriously offers himself nevertheless as a guide to life. "A philosopher cannot wish," he says, "to be deceived. His philosophy is a declaration of a policy in the presence of the facts." That he has been tempted merely to enjoy rather than to journey we know from his askances aimed at others. "Poets and philosophers sometimes talk as if life were an entertainment, a feast of ordered sensations; but," throwing himself reluctantly against this disavowal of responsibility, he goes on, "the poets, if not the philosophers, know too well in their hearts that life is no such thing: it is a predicament. We are caught in it; it is something compulsory, urgent, dangerous, and tempting. We are surrounded by enormous, mysterious, only half-friendly forces." Nor can any degree of progress make it less imperative for us to utilize for life whatever guidance is available. "We are not less dependent than our forefathers on food, on circumstances, on our own bodies." Since then, as he teaches, philosophy has its proper place in daily life, we follow one who believes in his leadership, whatever may be the outcome. We can rest in the needed assurance that we are not judging one seriously when

he was really merely amusing himself and
challenging us with amiable banter.

I

In order not to do Santayana the injustice
of making him appear fantastic, we must see
that he is not equally monarch of all the
territory which he surveys. There is no
phase of life's experience that he has not
done something to describe. In surveying all
realms of being, as a philosopher may, he
distinguishes the realm of matter, the realm
of spirit, and the realm of essence. If he hesi-
tates to announce himself a guide in the first
realm, it is not merely that he confesses a
greater degree of ignorance in regard to matter than some other men feel obliged to confess, but also that he presumes himself to
put first things first in the ordering of life.

The realm of matter is what common
sense supplemented by the several natural
sciences reveals it to be. The fact that knowledge of it can never be absolute, that matter
itself can never be known in any intimate
and final sense, does not disturb him. After
all, as he says, knowing is not eating. Few
philosophers, if any, have ever lived who

were more averse to using the fragmentariness of our knowledge about nature to justify some idealistic rendering of it that would conjure away its sharp corners and flatter the human spirit with honeyed words as to either the inner friendliness of nature or as to its own final supremacy over natural forces. "I stand in philosophy," he says, "exactly where I stand in daily life; I should not be honest otherwise." Common sense reveals nature to be a meadow in which both grass and thorns grow, in which flowers and weeds alike thrive, in which life develops and death is universal and sure. Nothing of this is blinked by Santayana. Indeed all is admitted, and life must be oriented with reference to this realm of inexorable matter.

"A philosopher cannot wish to be deceived . . . . and therefore his first care must be to ascertain and heartily to acknowledge all such facts as are relevant to his action or sentiment . . . . a philosopher may well love truth for its own sake, in that he is disposed to confront destiny, whatever it may be, with zest when possible, with resignation when necessary, and not seldom with amusement." If philosophy is not quite so frequently invoked in the realm of matter as in other realms, it is because in the partitioning that language makes necessary in the life of reason, science and common sense are assigned this realm as their special domain. The final word of practical wisdom would be the attainment on the common-sense level of an adjustment between wants and nature. Animals have, in this regard, been more fortunate than man; for "they have had time," as he says, "to take the measure of life, and have settled down to a routine of preferences and habits which keeps their heads, as a race, above water." Men, on the other hand, turn fruitlessly from one panacea to another, "impatient of being so long the sport of divers ignorant dogmas and chance adventures, and aspire to live in a stable harmony with nature."

Unless, however, the philosopher aspires no higher than the bovine level, facts and the realm of facts cannot represent his ultimate ambition, "although he must wish to know the whole unvarnished truth about relevant matters." This is an essentially animal level, and animal faith is the term that Santayana regularly uses to describe the technique of life on the physical plane. This verbiage is not meant to disparage human life as animal activity. All that science can do is none too much to be done for easing our way among the crags and bogs of matter. Santayana cannot belittle the physical aspect of life, as philosophers have habitually done; because he assumes not merely that this is one true realm of being but that it constitutes the substructure of the realm of spirit. But all that can be done to facilitate our animal living is not enough to beguile the soul to content itself exclusively with this realm. "Existence would not be worth preserving if it had to be spent exclusively in anxiety about existence." Matter points in man to spirit. "Spirituality has succeeded in adding consciousness without confusing instinct." "It is only for the sake of this free life that material competence and knowledge of fact are worth attaining. Facts for a living creature are only instruments; his play-life is his true life."

> Nature hath not made us, like her other children,
> Merely for peopling of her spacious kingdoms,
> Beasts of the wild, or insects of the summer,
>   Breeding and dying,

But also that we might, half knowing, worship
The deathless beauty of her guiding vision
And learn to love, in all things mortal, only
      What is eternal.

II

And so, quitting the realm of matter,
where philosophy is animal faith—at best
science, otherwise just common sense—we
achieve the realm of spirit, where the philosopher may put on his purple and sit down to
feast his soul. As he has been our guide heretofore by bidding us attend
      those obstinate questionings
    Of sense and outward things,
so now he will be our host while we joyously
contemplate
      those first affections,
    Those shadowy recollections,
    Which, be they what they may,
  Are yet the fountain-light of all our day,
  Are yet a master-light of all our seeing.

It is, however, well for us to remember that
we have not reached our second realm by
invalidating the first. We remain circum-
scribed by matter, but while in it we are not
wholly of it. Indeed before we fully compre-

hend the stern stresses that led us as children of nature to subordinate beauty to truth in finding our way about, we had tasted the fruits of fancy. "Fine art is . . . . older than servile labour, and the poetic quality of experience is more fundamental than its scientific value." Let us orient ourselves in this airy land, for this is life at its best and our host and guide is its prophet. We must keep our bearings: below us, as it were, lies the realm of matter in which at meal time and work time we still grope our way; above us, as it were, lies the realm of essence, in which all that spirit encompasses was, is, and still will be when matter masters spirit.

Seen from this high vantage of the life of spirit, "the human scene itself is," as he says, "but a theme for reflection."

> It is my crown to mock the runner's heat
> With gentle wonder and with laughter sweet.

This vantage point was clearly not achieved without travail. Santayana's leadership, like that of every man whose science is all art, is available only for those who in moments of imaginative insight can recapitulate his travail. That America is not the

most ready spot for his aesthetic interpretation of life might be inferred, did we not
know it independently by Santayana's willing and permanent absence from America.
He came to us after the emotional strands
of his soul had already been formed; he left
us before his mature powers were coining
themselves into his ripest reflections upon
the several realms of being. The roots of
American life, as he remarks of the English
language, did not quite "reach to his centre."
Here he found a race that "seldom has leisure to dwell on essences apart from their
presumable truth; even their beauty and
dialectical pattern seem rather trivial, unless
they are significant of facts in the realm of
matter, controlling human destiny." This
"tragic segment of the realm of essence" he
has called the realm of truth. Against this
aspect of American life, Santayana always
rebelled, even while he was among us. In
some of its forms it appeared to him comic,
in others tragic; but whether seducing smiles
or tears, the overemphasis upon action and
the overdevotion to success continually
struck him as preoccupation with less than
the best.

My heart rebels against my generation,
That talks of freedom and is slave to riches,
And, toiling 'neath each day's ignoble burden,
Boasts of the morrow.

No space for noonday rest or midnight watches,
No purest joy of breathing under heaven!
Wretched themselves, they heap, to make them happy,
Many possessions.

Caught nevertheless in the midst of his generation, unable wholly to gain detachment from it, more unable still to sink himself in its distractions, in one of his early poems he gives a disillusioned picture of himself as he stands upon the threshold of manhood, discouraged with his youth now past, unexpectant of better things from approaching maturity.

Such is youth:
Till from that summer's trance we wake, to find
Despair before us, vanity behind.

How much of the strife expressed in Santayana's early verse is literary, is vicarious, is indeed whimsical, one does not know for certain. That it is dramatically sincere no one doubts; and that there is now and again poignancy in it no sensitive reader can question. How out of the conflict between himself and his environment, or to speak more accurately, between two parts of himself, he was able finally to weave a character as beautifully integrated as his mature work reveals, we can only conjecture. But a conjecture upon this significant enigma is worth more in evaluating one who offers himself as our guide than a parade of other less meaningful facts. Perhaps it was the grace of Harvard University in offering this exotic character first a job and through rapid recognition a profession respectable by prevailing standards and yet isolated from the scramble of the market-place. Perhaps it was some heroic inner renunciation this side of the monastery that gave him peace. Or may it have been an entirely independent discovery of some golden fountain of energy and strength within himself that sang itself out in prose no less than in verse?

> Heaven it is to be at peace with things:
> Come chaos now, and in whirlwind rings
> Engulf the planets, I have seen the best.

However it may have been, he achieved a harmony of himself and with it a peace of mind that was matched by kindliness, good humor, and tolerance toward others that made and make him the genial teacher of a growing number of Americans. Few philosophers have been more cosmopolitan than is Santayana. His style achieves concreteness and great beauty almost wholly without local color. From everywhere, from nowhere, he beckons us unto the realm of spirit.

> And in eternal quiet float and soar:
> Where all my loves are gathered into one,
> Where change is not, nor parting any more,
> Nor revolution of the moon and sun.

This realm of spirit we must now explore for ourselves; and from it, once understood and evaluated, we must reach forth with our guide to appropriate at last the realm of essence. Perhaps our best approach is through what Santayana has called the "tragic Realm of Truth." As animals who must stake their fortunes and also their lives upon ideas, otherwise upon something more precarious still, men must set the greatest stead upon truth. Ideas are true, to put it as simply as possible, when they really represent what they purport to represent. If they are false, they may well be our ruin, since after we have followed their lead, it is often-times too late to retrace our steps. But whether false or true, they *are*. What they *represent* is one thing, supremely important for an animal; what they *are* is another thing, and the first thing for spirit. Since they are themselves something quite inde-pendent of what they represent, they may be taken for what they are rather than for what they mean or signify in action. So to take them is to gain a realm above matter, and so to live is to live spiritually.

That all men can so live is indicated by the fact that its knowledge side does not ex-haust any idea. "Existence may revert at any moment to play, or may run down in idleness; but it is impossible that any work or discovery should ever come about without the accompaniment of pure contemplation, if there is consciousness at all; so that the inherent freedom of the spirit can never be stamped out, so long as spirit endures." Even the humblest sensation is something in its own right as well as something by proxy. "The knowledge . . . . of relevant truth . . . . is far from being our only con-

cern in the life of reason. It comes in only
incidentally, in so far as a staunch and comprehensive knowledge of things makes a man
master of things, and independent of them
in a great measure. The business of a philosopher is rather to be a good shepherd of his
thoughts." Who does not know from the
simplest experience that fancy overflows the
narrow boundaries of utility even where one
must devote himself sharply to the job at
hand? While it is true that in some vague
general sense, fitness in ideas as well as elsewhere has a survival value, there is a wide
tolerance of error. As Santayana so well
states the matter, "The control which the
environment exercises over the structure
and conduct of animals is decidedly loose.
They can live dragging a long chain of idle
tricks, diseases, and obsolete organs; and
even this loose control fails almost entirely
in the case of alternative sense or languages,
one of which may serve as well as another."
Though undoubtedly nature exercises in the
long run a control in the field of ideas as well
as elsewhere, nevertheless in any short run
she drives, as Santayana observes, "with a
loose rein, and vitality of any sort, even if

expressed in fancy, can blunder through many a predicament in which reason would despair."

This overflow of animal vitality in every act of fancy but attests the presence of spirit throughout the broadened stretch of animal faith. One has but to recognize its presence, prize its function, and hold it for its superior worth, to rise from brute to man and from man to mind. What vistas are unfolded, what freedom is won, what peace is secured when "this world of free expression, this drift of sensations, passions, and ideas, perpetually kindled and fading in the light of consciousness" is taken as the heritage of the spirit! Though swinging in and out of ken, the objects of spirit are each and all in passing what they are, having neither implications nor consequences. Through identifying ourselves momentarily with this concourse, we justify the energy that the animal level has transmuted for our spiritual use and immortalize ourselves through preoccupation with the immortal.

> we behold, from those eternal towers,
> The deathless beauty of all winged hours,
> And have our being in their truth alone.

To take the stream of consciousness in this wise is not the easiest thing for spirit that draws its sustenance from animal activities in a precarious world. But for the welcome ally that science has become in freeing mind from matter through mastery of the latter, only a sparse spiritual life would be possible for men. With this freedom, not all difficulties vanish. Men get enmeshed in the machinery of freedom itself, and lose their souls in the process of emancipation. Since all ideas do have backgrounds and foregrounds, assumptions and implications; and since these can be appropriated for animal needs, a discipline is demanded whereby mind may free itself from memory and anticipation and find itself in the immediacy of contemplative imagination.

The primary discipline for the safeguarding and increasing of what Santayana calls the "freedom of the spirit" is skepticism. Not until men know what they can and what they cannot indubitably know will they prize as final the first fruits of spirit. Unlike the father of modern skepticism and of modern philosophy as well—Descartes, who found his doubting allayed when he

came upon himself, the doubter, *dubito ergo
sum*—Santayana makes a clean sweep. "I
shall deny," says he, "the existence of
everything, and abolish that category of
thought altogether. If I could not do
this, I should be a tyro in skepticism.
Belief in the existence of anything, in-
cluding myself, is something radically in-
capable of proof, and resting, like all belief,
on some irrational persuasion or prompting
of life." Finding "ultimate skepticism precious to a spiritual mind, as a sanctuary from
grosser illusions," Santayana erases time and
space, God and freedom, matter and mind,
soul and sense: ."nothing given exists." He
makes a clean sweep—almost. Existence is
all gone, but existence is not the only realm
of being. For the province of matter animal
faith must modestly count as knowledge;
but beyond matter there is left for spirit a
realm indubitable. "When by a difficult sus-
pension of judgment," Santayana concludes
his adventure into skepticism, "I have deprived a given image of all adventitious significance, when it is taken neither for the
manifestation of a substance nor for an idea
in a mind nor for an event in a world, but

simply if a colour for that colour and if music for that music, and if a face for that face, then an immense cognitive certitude comes to compensate me for so much cognitive abstention. My skepticism at last has touched bottom, and my doubt has found honourable rest in the absolutely indubitable."

This realm of essence upon which we have now come is a gorgeous fairyland of childhood, a magic land for all the seven ages of man. No person is so poor that he cannot, be he but awakened to his own resources and disciplined to appropriate them,

> in a moment travel thither,
> And see the Children sport upon the shore,
> And hear the mighty waters rolling evermore.

All this infinite diversity, beauty, and richness for the price of an imagination disciplined to penetrate beyond the utility of mere existence! Here we have awaiting us content for a purely aesthetic way of life. Self-mastery remains, however, the price of admission. No new heaven is to be opened up for free settlement by the world-weary. Nor is there here any berth for sloth; no insurance for the tender-minded. Indeed as mind arises from a happy affinity of atoms, so mind with all its proliferations as spirit passes away with the dissolution of its material basis. Our guide holds with Rupert Brooke that

these shall pass,
Whatever passes not, in the great hour,
Nor all my passion, all my prayers, have power
To hold them with me through the gate of Death.
They'll play deserter, turn with the traitor breath,
Break the high bond we made, and sell Love's trust
And sacramented covenant to the dust.

Such is the human part in all this fair territory now to be indicated and extolled by our guide. Seeing him unmoved, however, over the prospect of mortal dissolution at the very gates of Elysium, we abate our own perturbation until we find the undisclosed secret of his composure. Let us now enter with our guide the realm of essence and see what there we find.

III

We have seen that while ideas are more than stimuli, more than indications for action, they nevertheless are that. "They may," as Santayana says, "become terms in knowledge if interpreted judiciously, and if interpreted injudiciously they may become illusions." To know that one's ideas are adapted to conduct, one must know more than ideas; he must know life. Partly out of need for knowledge, therefore, arose this doctrine of essence. What we possess in imagination, while real enough, is not substantial enough for animals. Ideas represent real things, however; else we could not attribute to them a truth value. But how can we know that on the animal level there are any real things to which they correspond? If the parallelism is not complete so that in knowing ideas we also immediately know things, then we do not know things at all, but just ideas. If we do not know *what* things are, how do we know *that* they are at all? Perhaps the realm of imagination is after all the real world and there is in truth no realm of matter. Thus skepticism to every real thinker, as we have seen to Santayana.

One way of refuting this conjectural idealism is evolutionary materialism; and earlier at least Santayana seems to have availed himself of it. One might hold that since the level of matter came first and life and mind arose through a natural process out of it,

their potencies must be measured in terms
of it. Ideas can rise no higher than their
source. Hence ideas are always projects of
the world of matter, the needs of the organ-
ism, and have their only significance in the
modifications of the environment which has
travailed to bring them forth. They must
truly represent the environment; otherwise
they would not be. In his earlier work, *The
Life of Reason*, the processes of nature, of
society, of art, of religion, seem to pitch
ideas up in their churning, as the surging
ocean brings to birth the iridescent foam.
First the uselessness of this ideational foam
invites philosophic wonder; but ideas have
great utility when they are used as instruments of animal adjustment. Nevertheless,
there remains always a margin of inutility,
which is nevertheless real. Wherein does its
reality lie? It is this question that seems to
have intrigued Santayana himself, though
the other question as to the relation of ideas
to things has intrigued many of his disciples
and collaborators in the development of critical realism, with which his name is associated.

Ideas, while not the very things of nature,

are held to be the essence of the things for which they stand. They have the rare quality of being directly known by mind; and while in some eager moment we might wish knowledge to be such intimacy as that we could actually engorge the world of nature in the act of knowing, nevertheless for the most part all we need and care to know is the essence of things. If ideas are by definition the essences of things, we can by the certitude of definition vouch for the knowledge of nature afforded through them. This verbal facility touches a poet more sensitively, no doubt, than it would a scientist, though it must be said that Santayana takes all such speculations with sanity and humor. Freed thus from the necessity of consulting their constituency, ideas become lords; and we inherit as the ripest fruit of speculative ingenuity an upper house for the realm of spirit. But if essences are pitched up, as are ideas, by the revolutions of matter, they may be as evanescent, as episodic, as is the foam of the sea. Natural things are subject to the course of nature. Things of beauty should not always be passing; they should remain and abide.

The maturer work of Santayana has marked progressive emphasis upon such a view of essences as would give a permanence and immortality to them, so that they would be neither generated from nor doomed with the evanescence of things. If while remaining the essences of natural objects and therefore the instruments of knowledge when animal need presses for satisfaction, they could be completely validated as real in their own right, something would be saved from the all-engulfing sea of change. Just as the representative character of ideas for scientific use does not exhaust ideas, so the ideational character of essences does not exhaust them. Nor is their eternal nature in any sense impaired by the psychological use to which they are subject. Infinite in number, diverse in quality, variegated in form, they represent the sum-total of all that ever has been or can possibly come to be. Though the ideas which they upon occasion inform have themselves a natural history in terms of the life and need of the body, essences have not been derived from any evolutionary process, nor do they lose one iota of their significance by functioning as ideas in the vital flux.

Things no more exhaust ideas than do ideas exhaust essences. Useless though not worthless, they are; to discover them is to rise to the realm of spirit, and to treat them as of supreme worth is to identify oneself with eternal values.

There are ways and ways, however, of taking essences. One may take them, as we have seen in chapters iii and iv, in the scientific fashion and make of them hypotheses for experimentation or programs for conduct. This is to catch their mental shadows rather than themselves, and is to get from what is itself useless some large measure of utility. This is to be encouraged, of course; but it is not to be misunderstood. Science does not in any sense exhaust the possibilities of life, any more than it exhausts the nature of the essences. Science offers no final way of life except for those too easily satisfied. These essences may be taken in a religious fashion, as we have seen in chapter ii. It may be thought that they, when properly christened, are themselves potent to enforce ideals upon nature. So to take them is to prove oneself not religious but superstitious, and mercenary as well. It is to debase things eternal in their dignity and nature to mere means for personal profit. Religion for the noble mind must have a far worthier motive than this: the motive of assimilating oneself, through contemplation, to the things eternal, rather than of using these eternal verities to improve earthly fortune. In his *Platonism and the Spiritual Life* Santayana has related the whole tradition of supernaturalism, represented among us by Christianity, to Plato's mistake in raising moral and aesthetic essences into exclusive pre-eminence. The true spiritual life is not appropriation of values in this material sense, but is so complete a "disintoxication from values," to use Santayana's phrase, as will enable one to enjoy in contemplation, without expectation of returns, whatever essences may majestically swim into his ken.

So to live is in all truth to exemplify the aesthetic way of life, a way that gives the rapt self but does not expect to get anything from the giving, a way of life which cannot lead to disillusion and disappointment because it looks for nothing from life except the mere living of it imaginatively: "for," as Santayana rhetorically queries, "after life is done, and the world is gone up in smoke, what realities may the spirit of man boast to have embraced without illusion, save the very forms of these illusions by which he has been deceived?" Recognizing the superiority of this austerely sensuous way, at once Stoic and Epicurean, we shall count our science for what it is worth in making possible the continuation of life. We shall not, however, sink ourselves in merely living, but shall still seek a life.

God who gives the bird its anguish maketh nothing manifest
But upon our lifted foreheads pours the boon of endless quest.

But in our quest, we must not look beyond essences for powers or persons; we must not look below essences for material things; but we must look at essences, and achieve through vision our emancipation.

IV

Who is not in a glow from surveying such landscape with such a guide! From the cramped quarters of our hotel, we have skirted the blue Mediterranean of mind, and then proceeded exuberantly to the airy Alps.

From the chilly austerity of snow-capped heights, we have taken the wings of metaphysical fancy and sojourned a quiet hour with eternal essences. And then back from essence to mind and from mind to matter we have come. Here we are again at our own habitat. No gratuity is asked by our guide; the trip was for him its own reward. We must now eat, and soon to bed, and tomorrow to work again. All the other animals also eat and sleep and squander their energies in activity.

Animal faith must unquestionably in the future as in the past furnish us our basic equipment for living. If we live our animal life healthily and without shame, the life of reason rises slowly under wise nurture from instinct to spirit.

> Our knowledge is a torch of smoky pine
> That lights the pathway but one step ahead
> Across a void of mystery and dread.
> Bid, then, the tender light of faith to shine
> By which alone the mortal heart is led
> Unto the thinking of the thought divine.

This faith of Santayana's youthful muse has grown into the intuition of his maturity, which is, as he conceives it, a direct apprehension of essences. The life of a disciplined imagination is the spiritual life. This is not a discipline of renunciation but of judicious appropriation—appropriation at last of the essences but of them through robust living on all levels. One cannot become spiritual by renouncing knowledge, though spirituality is more than intellectuality; nor can he become wise through abstinence, though wisdom implies self-control. The ideal life is one in which nothing is lost. The full life, not the empty life, is the life to live. Civilization, primarily through science, is making that life possible for more and more people. It is only as men are freed from enforced preoccupation with bodily needs that mind can greatly matter to them; and it is only as they are in like manner emancipated from concern with the truth value of ideas that they can appreciate duly the essences which ideas body forth. Reminiscent of Plato, and far more than most philosophers since Plato, Santayana counsels sagely upon the conduct of life.

The secret of his wisdom lies in this: he knows the weakness of philosophy and avoids it; he knows the strength of philosophy and

develops it. He sees that philosophy is but
a literary anticipation of science, that metaphysics can neither supplant nor supplement
physics, and that ethics can do no better
than harmoniously to organize whatever
vital resources we have. Upon the death of
a metaphysician, Santayana celebrates the
virtue of philosophic modesty:

I stood and saw you fall, befooled in death,
As, in your numbed spirit's fatal swoon,
You cried you were a god, or were to be;
I heard with feeble moan your boastful breath
Bubble from depths of the Icarian sea.

Profiting from his ironic observation of
others, he does not even squander pages, as
is the contemporary wont, in disguising his
ignorance of nature through an elaborate
emphasis upon emergence. Unashamed of
common sense, he takes as philosophic realms
the levels of emergence that it distinguishes.
Relegating to science the realm which it
alone can handle, Santayana elaborates the
levels that a literary artist can illuminate.
He sees, too, what is highly important for
life at every stage, that no higher level takes
anything from the lower level. It, rather,
adds something to it. The traditional as-

sumption that to gain one we must renounce the other, leads to loss of both. With Browning, Santayana wholesomely advises:

> Let us not always say
> "Spite of this flesh today
> I strove, made head, gained ground upon the whole!"
> As the bird wings and sings,
> Let us cry "All good things
> Are ours, nor soul helps flesh more, now, than flesh helps soul!"

Santayana's goods have the characteristic emphasized by all moralists as distinguishing final values—they are non-competitive: for one to get more does not mean for others to get less. But our guide has little of the intolerance that characterizes professional moralists. The goods of mind are sharable without diminution, and each person may take his choice. The essences are infinite, are available for all minds, and are not consumed in contemplation.

Economic goods are lessened for some by others getting more; but an aristocracy of the spirit need not monopolize all the economic goods. In fact the material possession necessary for spiritual health is much less than is thought necessary by our civilization.

Moreover, Santayana emphasizes science as much as any; and science is the means for releasing men from preoccupation with acquisitiveness so that they may nevertheless build spiritual prosperity upon material assurance. Here, then, is a philosophy which while in essence aesthetic, does not overlook other goods. It urges complete and discerning appropriation of all of them. While it does not preach the rights of man, there is involved in it an elemental sense of justice that all men should partake of all goods up to the full level of their capacity. The emphasis upon material goods as basic, but not final, leaves open and desirable such a distribution of them as makes possible the fullest sharing of non-competitive goods. As the aesthetic quality of ideas represents an exuberance over their truth value, so what aristocracies may with justice appropriate must represent a surplus of nature and of human society that but for the favored classes would remain inchoate or actually go to waste. That no historic aristocracy has been content to let others have the power and the goods if only it might contemplate the essences, while justly arousing democratic suspicion, does not prove the unwisdom of Santayana's vision. This genial guide has not only expressed but has also seemed to practice the maxim: give me the luxuries and I will not grieve for the necessities. To see that the best of life, like the essences, can be had without being possessed and to live life in this recognition, is to live it in wisdom and in peace.

CHAPTER VI
THE PHILOSOPHIC WAY OF LIFE WITHOUT A GUIDE

There was a time when in the teeth of fate
I flung the challenge of the spirit's right;
The child, the dreamer of that visioned night,
Woke, and was humbled unto man's estate.

—SANTAYANA

WE HAVE now become familiar with the idea that the speculations of philosophers, whatever tone they may take, are adjustments to life which certain men have found satisfactory and which after trial they soberly recommend to others. The diversity of their reactions but serves to show how variegated are the needs and temperaments of men. A Royce sees in the universe a call to loyalty and adoration. He expresses this attitude, and we are richer by one philosophy. A James sees in it a challenge to initial adventure and to eventual improvement. He publishes this in a book, and we are richer by two philosophies. A Dewey feels the needs of men, preoccupies himself with a more humane social order, thinks out loud about it, and we are richer by three philosophies. A Santayana sees in the universe an opportunity for animal contentment and for spiritual peace. He articulates an attitude, generalizes it, and we are richer by four philosophies.

So it goes: age cannot wither, nor custom stale man's infinite variety. To study other men's philosophies is merely ornamental, however, unless it helps one to grow a philosophy of his own. For philosophy is not primarily knowledge, it is wisdom. Wisdom is knowledge utilized for life and action. Since no one can live life for another, no one however great can philosophize adequately for another however humble. Each man has his own chapter to write in the genuine story of philosophy. At his peril he fails to write into this story his own vision of life and the world; for the world as he sees it *is* his soul. What will a man give in exchange for his soul?

I

This insistence that every man have a philosophy of his own helps to dissipate a

not insignificant obstacle to every man's getting a better philosophy than he has. The
obstacle is the belief that only great men
have philosophy and that they can furnish
it ready-made to humbler men. No man can
wholly appropriate another's point of view.
If so, nature had best make but one man
grow where two grew before. To be a person
means to have some unique slant, which
should be the priceless core of that person's
philosophy. To seek to satisfy oneself with
another's vision is to make even more fatal
than it need be the overspecialization of
modern life.

That overspecialization with its impover-
ishment of versatility constitutes at bottom
this obstacle to the philosophic way of life.
In order to live at all in our world, one must
accept most of his goods without experienc-
ing and so without understanding the process that produces them. They come to us
from unknown persons as end-products of
activities little understood. The only fruitful test as to whether a commodity is a
"good" is indeed whether it is worth the
price of production. That we are deprived of
knowing, since we know neither the process

nor the producers. Reduced to the necessity of taking ready-made most of the commodities on which we live, we find it easy to satisfy ourselves with second-hand experience. If the highly specialized movie stars can furnish us our love and our morals, why not the wise men our philosophy? Since, too, the philosopher lives in a specialized age, what is his function unless he can furnish to others some ready-to-wear garment? That specialization represents a gain for efficiency goes without saying, but whether it constitutes a gain for human happiness depends primarily upon the discovery of a way to unite again our dissevered experiences. How to achieve generalized wisdom in a highly specialized age?

It is certain that a man cannot achieve his unity by actually going through the specialized processes that in our time converge upon him as consumer. Since he cannot *work* them together, the only hope is that he can still *think* them together. Thinking manipulates symbols of things. Philosophy is the ancient name for the human attempt to grasp the universe by proxy, and thus to see life steady and keep it whole.

There is a modern definition of philosophy which seriously conceives it as "the attempt to go from the known to the unknown by means of words." Since philosophy is the idea-way of life and thinking itself is a substitute for thicker and fuller experiences, philosophy at the best is one remove from reality. When Plato, the first great Western philosopher, turned from speculation in the Academy to administration at Syracuse, he declared that he did so from a concern for his own self-respect: "I feared to see myself at last altogether nothing but words." The fact, however, that one must get one remove from reality in order to encompass it should not be used to justify the process of removal ad infinitum. Thinking about things may have great utility, whereas thinking about thought may have very little utility. For one to take his philosophy ready-made is for him to be two removes from reality. Plato objected to certain forms of art upon the ground that they were thrice removed from reality. Two removes is too much for philosophy.

Both because the philosopher as intellectually specialized wishes to dispose of his wares and because common men as otherwise specialized have no facility at judging his wares, stale philosophy is more common than stale bread. But men can have their own ideas even when they cannot own anything else. Indeed, they should insist upon having their own ideas: ideas sometimes lead to more substantial things. Meanwhile, they can help to compensate for other lacks and especially for the lack of wholeness produced by specialization. Words are not the whole of life; but it is better to talk about life than to do nothing about it. A report, however, upon a reported report is not as significant for life as a report upon a report, and that not as significant as a report upon life itself. A philosophy of life based upon philosophy is not as valuable as a philosophy of life based upon life itself. To take life without a guide means to become one's own guide. This involves a great responsibility, but not so great a responsibility as the self-surrender involved in following another unquestioningly.

In a world of limited goods, some men's desires get better satisfied by renunciation on the part of others. Renunciation comes to be taught as the easiest method of social control. Once men are led to believe that they are better for doing without things, others can dominate them and enjoy their birthright with impunity. Let no one ever doubt that this is normally the result of discipline. The good child is the one who lets parents and teachers lead their own lives unmolested. Once men get socially implanted the metaphysical principle upon which Royce and other religious philosophers build, a dominant group is assured of its prerogatives. For if the reality of things is constituted by their inclusion in a class above them, then the legitimacy of personal wants and the opportunity of social classes are defined in the same way. If a person must learn what his rights are, what his duty, by asking some superior person, it does not take a wise man to know who will get the best of that relationship.

Ideas are the one thing most easy for men to have; they are the one thing most dangerous not to have; let us therefore get ideas and direct our own expedition into life. Before we can effectively do so, however, we must overcome two great dogmatisms: the dogmatism of others which urges us to take their thoughts without criticism; the dogmatism of ourselves which urges us to take our own thoughts without criticism from others. We may profitably comment further upon these two hindrances to the philosophic way of life.

II

One must constantly be on his guard against the air of finality carried by many idea-systems. Not all philosophical systems have claimed to be final, though all too many of them have so claimed. Short of the overt claim, however, there is the connotation of conclusiveness that hangs around all finished work, especially around all written work. The order of logic is not the order of thinking, but the reverse. One thinks tentatively and fumblingly. He puts the cart before the horse, then the horse before the cart facing it, then the cart behind the horse. But when he writes up his trip, he hitched the horse to the cart and drove off—just like that! Finished work daunts thinking; it invites contemplation. To begin always at the end is eventually to doubt the worth-whileness of beginning at all. It is to invite one to appropriate the work of another and thus to forfeit the performance of his own work; for it is not to get the problem, it is to get the solution. Solutions may be well for enjoyment, but they are not useful to one who seeks a way to live and work. Why work, indeed, when the product has been already finished? The answer is, of course, that the work that has been done is the other man's work, not one's own at all. To suppose it to be one's own work is to daunt endeavor, stifle individuality, and deprive mankind of whatever variety and novelty each person possesses by being an individual. It is, in short, to regiment thought or action or feeling. This is precisely what most theologies and metaphysics and art systems have done, as we may see with a moment's reflection.

Theologians have claimed to offer a way of salvation already finished, which could be appropriated merely by an act of faith on the part of the elect. It has always been a way so good that nobody could on his own equal it. So it was not only offered, it must be accepted. "I am the way, the truth, and the life; no man cometh unto the Father, but by me." "If your women will learn any-

thing, let them ask their husbands at home."
"If any man preach any other gospel unto
you than that which we have preached unto
you, let him be accursed." "If any man shall
add unto these things, God shall add unto
him the plagues that are written in this
book." And so, furnished with a ready-made
way of life, guaranteed to lead to salvation
for all because it has led to peace of mind for
the author, all other men are inhibited from
the only process through which growth and
personality completion can come—trial-and-
error experimentation. He who doubts is
damned already—this paralyzing dictum becomes the generalized anathema for those
who would begin their life at the beginning
rather than at what someone else found to be
for himself the end. One gets this dogmatic
attitude reflected, however, not only in
theologies but also in philosophies, as when
Royce warns men off skepticism by pointing
to pessimism; as when James equates ag-
nosticism with a loss of what willed belief
can recover; as when in popular philosophiz-
ing the "constructive" emphasis is the only
one commended. Against this whole attitude, it might be said at once, that he who

doubts not is fossilized already. No man can
profitably begin in thinking where another
man leaves off, unless he knows in advance
from where and how the other man came to
the conclusion.

To know this means, of course, that he
has already transcended the other thinker.
It is too obvious to permit emphasis, for instance, that the only way truly to imitate
Christ (that eidolon whom the race's dreams
have made) is to transcend Jesus, the historical character. To renounce confidence in
one's self is not to imitate one who boasted
complete self-confidence. The first step, likewise, in the Pauline way of life would consist
in asking Paul to get out of one's way. The
truly great soul, having appropriated all
others for his own growth, is willing to be
transcended by others for their growth—a
willingness indicated by neither of these
characters. "How prudently most men sink
into nameless graves, while now and then a
few forgot themselves into immortality."

Real thinking arises only from one's own
problems, not from another man's solutions
of his problems. The fatal thing about historic religions is their dominating drive back

to some authoritative person as source for a way of life. Vagueness alone makes historic characters acceptable to modern men as authoritative guides, as colorlessness makes political leaders acceptable to vested interests. Would it not conduce to clarity if men did as they pleased openly rather than under the forced interpretation of some other will than their own? Nor are the modern religions and the new-thought movements any better, save as getting nearer our own time they are more likely to lose the enchantment that distance gives such misty characters as Jesus, Buddha, Confucius. Only now word comes that Krishnamurti, the theosophical Messiah, has dissolved the Order of Star in the East, in the interest of freedom; but what led him to it was the fact that the order would not accept the truth (as *he* saw it, of course). There is really no hope in Messiahs unless each man become his own.

Perhaps nowhere, however, is the dogmatism implicit in finished work more dominating than in objects of art. Let us speak a word of the influence of non-literary works. Painting and sculpture set the perceptual forms of taste much as literary masterpieces set the conceptual forms of judgment. One dismisses, as Emerson says, "without notice his thought, because it is his." "Great works of art," he says in the same connection, "have no more affecting lesson for us than this. They teach us to abide by our spontaneous impression with good humored inflexibility, then most when the whole cry of voice is on the other side. Else, tomorrow a stranger will say with masterly good sense precisely what we have thought and felt all the time, and we shall be forced to take with shame our opinion from another."

If a person once comes to see the integration in an artist's own character that was achieved through a given work of art, he will discover at the same time that this is not precisely the integration that he himself needs. Appreciation of the work need not decline because of this; but the discovery should certainly lessen one's dependence upon another in matters of taste. An art that proliferates always from other works of art, like a philosophy that proliferates always from philosophies, is sure to end in formalism. Life and crude experience are the matrix, immediate or proximate, of all that is significant in ideas. When ideas inbreed, they eventuate in a progeny so delicate as prove sterile with their kind and unable to suffer the rude invigorating embrace of sons of the soil. Then arise new forms of art, of theology, of philosophy—a swarthier but robuster breed fresh from the fecund womb of Mother Nature. But cannot the old, the rarefied, the refined contribute something to the ever rising new forces? That depends largely upon the attitude of the old. It cannot transmit itself intact. What price will it pay for survival? There is potency in the old, in the achieved, in the matured, if it can but forswear dogmatism.

But there stands another type of dogmatism in the way of its assimilation. It is the dogmatism of the young and the provincial expressed in the belief that the old has nothing whatever to give. Not infrequently men think to build their own philosophies from the earth up, *de novo*. That they will miss something through this attitude, dogmatically held, seems certain. Ideas have some ability to fertilize ideas. As certain as that our study of these American philosophers cannot give us a finished philosophy of life is

the fact that our study of them can help us
to achieve a philosophy of life.

> I trace the lives such scenes enshrine,
> Give past exemplars present room,
> And their experience count as mine.

To explain how this is possible and thus to
mediate between the best of ideas that have
been and the best of ideas that may be would
be no thankless task.

That there are more things on earth than
we see, we all admit. That our lives are enlarged by the experiences we have, we know.
Since we see different things, we can lead
each other into new experiences. All conversation implies either that the parties to it
have had the same experiences and are com-
memorating their community or are giving
each other directions as to how to get new
experience. Communication becomes thus
either celebration or prediction. Philosophy,
we have seen, uses words as its medium. Let
us conceive all philosophy as a signboard:
"If you will go here or there," it seems to
say, "do thus or so, try this or that, you will
have such and such an experience. I tried it
and liked the experience, and I wish that you

might share my good fortune. If, however, you are really interested, do not take my word for it. The enjoyment I had was and is mine; I cannot give it you. You will have to achieve your enjoyment as I did mine by trying with open eyes the way of life that I indicate."

This gives written philosophy a rôle for those who are willing to experiment, but the experiment must always be re-enacted to get maximum results. Some things may be received on the word of others, as in science; but since this is always done at the peril of being taken in, one will in crucial cases perform the experiment for himself. To have experiments reperformed from time to time serves as a great precaution even in science; something may have been overlooked that itself is of more importance than the standard result. There is no guaranty that nature herself does not change from time to time; and since our "laws" are descriptions rather than prescriptions, they must be kept up to date. While this experimental view gives philosophy a rôle, it also supplies a standard for differential evaluation of various philosophies. Royce tells us, for example, that there is a spiritual mountain-top from which life looks much rosier than it otherwise appears. No one of us but that relishes the finest view of life that we can achieve. But can Royce tell us how to get to this magic mountain? Not precisely, for in truth he himself has never been there. It is the vantage point of Absolute Spirit. But Royce and we are not absolute.

Had he seen God, to write so much of Him?

How does Royce know that there is such an Absolute Spirit? Well, *must* there not be such, for otherwise life is doomed to fragmentariness and disillusion? When the basic reason for a belief is that it *must* be true, the man of wide experience will be on his guard lest the empty impetuosity of adolescence be inflicted upon him under the guise of religious loyalty or logical necessity. The logic of events will represent the mature man's only compulsion; and, as Walter Lippmann says in his *Preface to Morals*, the "imaginative understanding of that which is desirable in that which is possible" will represent the mature man's only devotion. But in so saying, I am exercising my temperamental prerogative to decline Royce's offer to be my guide. This right is the reader's also—with reference to me as well as to Royce. But I part with Royce reluctantly and only partly, even as I engage other guides circumspectly and for only part of the journey. I part with him because I am impelled to take a more scientific way, and being thus biased I find that through argument he would paralyze the nerve of effort. Experimenting with the scientific way, let us now see how much we can appropriate, how much we must exact, of the other ways of life. Our willing guides must at least not go unthanked.

III

Let me speak of the aesthetic way first since I have less to exact of, more to appropriate from, it. The head and front of our exaction of it is that useful actions and serviceable objects be not dogmatically excluded from the category of the beautiful. The monopoly by the fine arts of the rewards of beauty is as gross an offense against the scientific as against the democratic way of life. A dying feudalism has perpetrated no more ironic joke upon its conqueror than this presumed superior worth of useless objects and non-productive activities. The notion that an automobile or a shoe or a city apartment cannot be as beautiful as a painting or a sonata or a country house is a pathetic fraud. A fraud because it is an attempt on the part of a prestige class to maintain by indirection a supremacy that cannot be maintained directly; pathetic not merely because it ensnares the simple victims but eventually beguiles even the perpetrators into ignorance of the fact that their canons of taste have a natural history which renders them as relative to wont and use as is everything else. To an engineer nothing is more beautiful than a fine, efficient engine, and to the technical scientist nothing is more beautiful than the hypothesis that promises to sink itself through its own verification into hard fact or accepted law.

Once this exaction is acknowledged in good faith, the aesthetic attitude acquires a vast new accession. The prayer of M'Andrew in Kipling's "Hymn" is answered:

Lord, send a man like Robbie Burns to sing the Song o' Steam!

. . . .

Oh for a man to weld it then, in one trip-hammer
  strain,
Till even first-class passengers could tell the meanin'
  plain!
But no one cares except mysel' that serve an' under-
  stand
My seven thousand horse-power here. Eh, Lord!
  They're grand—they're grand!
Uplift am I? When first in store the new-made
  beasties stood,
Were Ye cast down that breathed the Word declarin'
  all things good?
Not so! O' that warld-liftin' joy no after-fall could
  vex,
Ye've left a glimmer still to cheer the Man—the
  Arrtifex!

The aesthetic way of life is called upon to
sacrifice its notion of the artistic superiority
of the useless, but it need not sacrifice the
useless itself. For once the notion of its differential value is given up, it acquires a use
in the life of mankind. Science does not
mean the death of poetry, even if it does
depreciate rhymed pomposity and metered
pretense. There is a poetry of common life,
of productive work, of useful things that he
might the better sing who knows them. This
prideless portrayal is a pean of

the very world, which is the world
Of all of us,—the place where, in the end,
We find our happiness, or not at all!

To recognize these as content for art is to put art in its true place in the life of mankind. If it must depend upon leisure for enjoyment, then it must recognize that leisure does not fall as the gentle rain from heaven upon the earth below. Leisure comes through control over nature and this means science and intelligence not ashamed of their tools or materials. But this would soon make obvious the truth that leisure is not the only condition of art. If utility may become the content of art, then utilitarian processes may themselves become artistic. If fine art lost its finery, it might gain substance. Art applied to action becomes artisanship, if the action move efficiently. The doing well of productive work is not merely content for art, it is art. There is no finer art than skilful artisanship. If this were once fully recognized, then the leisure necessary for the enjoyment of the type of art for which leisure is necessary would itself become possible for men in general, and thus the very art that fears for its life with every advance of technology would save its life by losing it. To seek immortality through isolation is a short-cut that cuts away the only chance at immortality—submergence in and appropriation by the great mass of humanity.

But to speak of short-cuts brings us back to humanity's institutionalized short-cut, religion. Of it we must ask all this and more if our preference for the scientific way of life is to prevail. And yet what we ask is not to be prematurely judged as unreasonable. We ask merely that religion free itself from superstition. We could not ask less; we need not ask more. To hypostatize ideas into powers is superstition if we then rely upon them as powers. To elevate ideas by personifying them as invisible allies is superstition if we then neglect other aids from confidence in them. Finally, to believe that the needs and desires of any number of men for anything establishes a ground for asserting that it exists or will eventually be forthcoming is the great parent superstition, if the ground for such belief be other than the energizing of nerves and muscles to make our desires come true. These, as we have earlier suggested, are religion's established techniques to success. Mr. George Santayana has from the aesthetic point of view, in his *Platonism and the Spiritual Life*, challenged religion to save its life by divorcing itself from superstition.

This same challenge we now issue also in the name of science. Since nobody has ever validated appeal to other than natural means by getting enough demonstrable efficacy from anything else to compete with natural means, we wish men to cease cheating themselves out of an indubitable minimum of concrete goods by affirming a spiritual maximum achievable through faith. What is more, we insist that coming generations shall not be called on to suffer evils as the result of our neglect to better them through putting our ideas to work. Faith might be an individual blessing if it did not prove a social curse. Since science needs all the human energy possible to effect the improvements that it envisages, luxuries can be denied the few in the name of necessities for all, even though the necessities be the humble ones of food, clothing, recreation, a modicum of leisure; and the luxury be that of robust faith in the providential governance of the universe. By law we have set a limit to the reach of Mormon faith in marital relations, by law we have narrowed the scope of Christian Science faith in the illusoriness of material things, when those things spread disease. Law is perhaps a poor weapon here. But by enlightened opinion we can discourage as a lazy vice any cosmic faith that detracts from any humblest piecemeal improvement of man's mundane habitat.

It is clear, then, that we propose for religion to content itself with a scientific and an aesthetic and a social emphasis. Ideas shall be treated as ideas and enjoyed for their beauty, or they shall be treated as projected patterns to be realized through co-operative exertions. We propose, moreover, that beauty in useless ideas and esoteric things shall not be put above, but kept below, that resulting from demonstrated utility. An image of an angel is not hereby interdicted, but preferential rating is given to the blue print of an engine that when finished will lessen the labor and increase the leisure of men. Leisure assured and distributed to all men, then images of angels may be enjoyed to one's heart's content. And this or any other activity may be called religious, so only the simple-minded be not beguiled from science and art by treating vicarious experience as a short-cut to power that can come only through knowledge and manipulation of natural means. It is noted, however, that perfectly good names already exist to describe the other realms, namely aesthetics and ethics and science. It is highly significant that the tendency in our generation to use religious categories to describe either physical processess or systems of ideas or experiences of beauty is largely restricted to those who earlier used the religious terms to connote persons or power that circumvented both ideas and things. This linguistic generosity is never wholly innocent. It is atavistic in import. But we shall not begrudge atavisms to such as find them necessary, if only they be enjoyed in leisure that has been personally acquired rather than socially inherited. We shall count them harmless only so long as they remain impotent. We shall tolerate impotence but shall encourage potency that comes from rediscovering to men virtues hidden by pious blindspots: the value of the precarious, the beauty of a stiff upper lip, the finality of a sense of humor.

Aristocracies have much to teach common men. Not least of their lessons is the value to life of strenuosity and danger. Sheltered through a long infancy by parents one of whom at least at the present halfway house of feminism is likely to convert industrially unengaged energy into maternal oversolicitude, the modern child, certainly of professional and wealthy parents, is too much shielded from the rougher corners of life. He easily becomes flabby: labor quickly degenerates into toil and exertion passes rapidly into pain. So conditioned, his contact with the strenuous but reinforces the implicit premise of his upbringing: ease and luxury are thought to constitute the only values of life. That they do not can easily be seen by an inspection of the life of those who inherit ease and luxury without having known enforced hardships. What they have escaped as necessity they seek oftentimes by choice. In sports and games and war they go in quest of the strenuous and find in the precarious compensation for the thinness of their lives. By contrast with its opposite, strenuosity acquires a positive value. Make more secure the lives of men, and they will not count insecurity so unmitigated an evil. The uncertainties of even the cosmic weather get wonderfully neutralized in the life of the scientist, of the explorer, of the human leader, and even of the fairly well-to-do city-dweller. It is poverty and isolation and impotence that invest with mortal terror many of the necessary vicissitudes of life.

But not all evils can be thus dismissed if one is to retain a sober sanity. It is a glory to poetry that Love cannot find Hell, as in Lanier's poem, or that, as in Hardy's, the Impercipient gazes unseeingly at the spiritual forms so familiarly hailed by his neighbors; but what means thus a halo for poetry spells a psychosis in the somber life of every day. This attitude which when idealized creates beauty and calls for praise, when realized creates a dissociation of personality and requires a priest or a physician. Pain may be called illusion, evil error, and death unreal; but pain still smarts, evil smites, and death destroys. Death in particular cannot be denied its place among ultimate earthly things. Persisting through all efforts to explain evil away or to ignore it, is a bitter residue that must be faced for what it is. How face this unambiguous residue? This question presses at last upon every man's philosophy of life. It drives most men to religion. It will be seen to budge us through science toward aesthetics.

IV

Conceivably one might face unpurged evil with a heroic, an undying protest. He might see pain and suffering, disappointment and death for what they are, but hold out resolutely against their injustice. Even though he should be forced to confess that about them he could do nothing, nevertheless there would remain to him the birthright of man, and he might refuse to stultify his soul by ignoring facts as they are or by calling them by names more gracious than their nature warrants. Living under a banner emblazoned with the motto of Thomas Hardy, "Truth will be truth alway," he might choose with other souls no less heroic than himself to march boldly against an invincible foe in a last battle the outcome of which is already decided against him. Upon

the firm foundation of unyielding despair, as
Bertrand Russell has suggested, he might
think adequately to build the soul's habita-
tion. Thus acts Prometheus in a good cause,
and Macbeth in a bad cause—if cause may
be bad in loyalty to which man never says
die. This attitude—it can hardly be called a
solution—never ceases to excite admiration;
it may indeed almost, if not quite, be called
the *sine qua non* of tragedy. Job has come
into undying fame through having maintained this attitude for a season; and Satan,
as Milton has drawn him, is the impersona-
tion of the tragic spirit in so far as he graced
his irremediable despair with unweakening
protest: "What though the field be lost, all
is not lost." This is the strenuous life, metaphysically illustrated. That man's spirit is
willing to take this route is indicated by the
aureoles with which human imagination has
invested such characters as these; but that
his flesh proves weak is also indicated by the
scarcity of bone-and-blood men who have
trodden this high road of heroic despair to
its very end. Where hope vanishes, there human resolution easily ends. However glori-
ously we may in the heyday of youth enroll

for the unending campaign, sooner or later under the withering compulsion of life's desert wastes or in the insidious loneliness of the night that closes in murkily on our latest defeat, most of us capitulate; and the terms of compromise mark the spot where the high resolves of gallant youth lie buried.

O it was easy in the morning dew
To make the vow that never should grow old,
But not at dusk, the words are not so bold—
Thus have I learned: how fares the hour with you?

Even Margaret Fuller at last accepted the universe.

But in the large there are at least two less strenuous ways of accepting the universe. The traditional way is that of resignation. When protesting has worn itself out against the world's most unyielding points, surrender comes creeping in as naturally as sleep follows a fatiguing day, or as dawn succeeds the passing night. There is a certain sense in which all obstacles cease to be obstacles when we take them into our idea-system and cease to struggle against them. Our enemies are enemies by our own grace as well as by their misconduct. As distinguished from the process of explaining evils away, resignation confesses them to exist, to exist as evils; and then ceases further to kick against the pricks. Since nothing *can* be done about them, *why* do anything? Patience lessens turmoil; and numbness commends itself above a sensitivity that does not avail.

> And at each cross I would surmise
> That if I had willed not in that wise
> I might have spared me many sighs.

There is no doubt a certain elemental economy of the emotional life in such reasoning. The path of resignation is worn by the footsteps of centuries. Its historical place as a Buddhistic and Stoic and Christian virtue may be taken as conclusive evidence as to the efficacy of resignation as one means of adjustment to such a world as this. It has opened a path of peace to countless harried souls. But its virtue has been also its defect. The personal peace that it brings is likely to be dearly paid for in the coin of social progress. Peace and progress are often as antithetical in fact as they are harmonious in sound. The reason lies at hand. Along with evils and goods, conceived as classes, there

always go many things not as good as one
could wish but not so bad as might be. Man's
attitude toward these evils-that-might-be-
made-goods determines their eventual status.
But this process of determination may be
hard enough to discourage endeavor; and,
what is more, it may be persistent enough to
outlast one or more generations. Moreover,
this ambiguous class is quite indefinite in
scope. Its boundaries are always changing
and are never precisely known even to the
wisest. Any attitude that accepts as irremediable what but for the acceptance were remediable is clearly dangerous to progress in
a dynamic world. Even if any situation can
be shown to be hopeless, resignation as a
way of accepting it so appeals to human inertia as constantly to tend to spread to what
is not at all irremediable, but is merely beyond easy remedy. An immaterial osmosis
motivated by inertia is too likely to infect
the whole of life. This seems to be precisely
what has traditionally happened where resignation has been generally acclaimed a virtue.

The Stoics, though formulating the bases
for an enlarged citizenship, were not them-

selves the best of citizens; for those classes of things that might have been made good by their efforts remained indifferent or even bad under the protection of their lethargy. It was insight into the insidiousness of another such easy way of dealing with a reluctant cosmos that led Plato into that immortal declaration of his faith in the efficacy of human effort.

"Some things," confesses Plato's Socrates, "I have said of which I am not altogether confident. But that we shall be better and braver and less helpless if we think that we ought to enquire, than we should have been if we indulged in the idle fancy that there was no knowing and no use in seeking to know what we do not know;—that is a theme upon which I am ready to fight, in word and deed, to the utmost of my power."

Early Christianity also set its seal upon resignation as a virtue. Placing their affections on things above, Christian saints have traditionally borne with patience conditions on earth that industry and courage would have changed for the better. The doctrine of non-resistance, the practice of indiscriminate charity, the emphasis put upon faith in an unchanging authority, and the assurance of other-worldly compensation—all these are but parts of the technique through which men have made this world bearable for themselves—but by which they also have left it unimproved for their children to bear. The logic of such an attitude is: If this condition be not of God, it will come to naught; if it be of God, we must not meddle. Therefore let us do nothing, not even seek to find whence it comes. Thus have men set up and worshiped the idol of indolence; and for a thousand years Western Europe reaped the inevitable results of such a spirit. Men cannot resign themselves to the evils of life wholesale without leaving future generations to pay wholesale retribution. Whether resignation arises after the order of early Christianity in the name of a universe so bad that human effort cannot prevail against it or after the order of Royce in the name of a universe already so perfect that nothing needs to be done about it as a whole, the concrete result is the same. The history of this conception has emboldened L. T. Hobhouse to say, "For collective mankind resignation is not a duty, but a coward's plea."

But to the social danger of resignation, historically illustrated by Stoicism and early Christianity, though remaining constant for all time, there is added the increasing unavailability of resignation as a means of adjustment for the modern man. The great historic religions have made resignation easy as an attitude by setting as a reward for indifference to the evils of life a great transcendental compensation. If resignation would not only lessen the pains of the present life—which it could certainly do—but would also serve as a sort of visé of one's passport to the islands of the blest, then were it easy indeed. The resignation of even Socrates had something of this support; for he was convinced, as he declared, that no harm can come to a good man, living or dead. But where resignation has to become in very truth its own reward; where after the resignation there remains nothing but the sufferer and the evil— hard indeed is then the lot of man. And this is the predicament that the modern man faces, even if he describe his attitude toward life as religious. For the religion of the modern man is cautious of promises for the future. The emphasis upon the present is as much an outgrowth of religion's uncertainty of the future as it is of its discovering an intrinsic value in the present. Religious liberals have discovered that the only basis that man ever had for assurance regarding the future is but the persisting desire to have the future rosy. And this has grown to seem an insufficient basis, since practically all human desires are thwarted partially and many of them completely. Indeed the discovery that the universe is indifferent to our desires save as they can *make* themselves effective, marks, as we have seen, the boundary between adolescence and maturity. The constant frustration of the very desires upon which hopes are built does not seem to provide sufficient reason for being dogmatic about the fulfilment of such desires.

Given, then, certain irremediable evils of life, resignation as a method of meeting them is not only socially harmful, but has the added disadvantage of being in modern times a very strenuous way. To resign oneself to evils where there is no ulterior recompense for the heroic act is much like falling back with assurance upon the motto, "Let justice be done though the heavens fall," when one actually knows that they will tumble down if he goes ahead. We shall then more easily admit that resignation is a moral anesthetic, needful in dire necessity, than that it is an unquestioned virtue for everyday living. So admitting, we shall without blame grant its easing power to individuals who suffer at the hands of life without other means of relief; but at the same time we shall register the need for a method of accepting the universe that will be more easily available for many and safer for all.

As affording such a method, there is another attitude that forms, in many ways at least, an active counterpart of the passive response connoted by resignation. Examples of this contrasting attitude are all about us, though for it we have as yet no universally accepted name. The playful might describe it as a sense of humor; the venturesome as sportsmanship; but the soberer mind would probably prefer to think of it as scientific curiosity. It is the attitude of the scientist while undergoing a painful experimentation, of the surgeon while performing a major operation upon himself, of the cheerful non-religious person in the last stage of tuberculosis, or of the philosopher suffering from an incurable cancer. Even the criminal who, eschewing all bitterness, dies "game" in some measure atones for his misdeed; and public opinion is quick to give him admiration whom it sent to the scaffold. There is no modern who would not be proud to number among his countrymen that intrepid Englishman who, although dying to gratify the whim of a monarch, could nevertheless say to his executioner: "Help me to ascend—I will shift for myself coming down." Passing by his fruitful life, Sir Thomas More signally served mankind in his death by thus immortalizing a new attitude toward what the situation made for him an irremediable evil.

Both the new and the old attitudes are alike those of a spectator; but resignation connotes a spectator who, fortified by visions of other and transcendental scenes his heart has conjured up, endures the game, though it is not to his liking. The scientific attitude, on the other hand, connotes a spectator who, though he likes not the game, knows that for the time being nothing else is available and so proceeds to interest himself in it. Even if nobody likes the game, not

even the players, still if all be forcibly de-
tained upon the field, it is the part of the
creative, as contrasted with the submissive
spirit, to manufacture an interest in the
process. Both attitudes involve detachment
also; but the one detaches magically by way
of another world, while the other leaves in
experience, for its enrichment, the technique
of detachment. This active acceptance of
the enforced rôle of spectator can go a long
way toward a constructive desensitizing of
human nature to the inexorable ills of life.
"The true unworldliness," as Santayana
says, "is knowledge of the world, not so
much a gaping and busy acquaintance as a
quiet comprehension and estimation which,
while it cannot come without intercourse,
can very well lay intercourse aside."

Resignation, passing through the valley
of tribulation, carries on because there is no
turning back or because the hills of bliss
gird the other side of the valley. It seems to
say, "If this strip of the journey were all,
then not to be were better than to be." It
confesses itself the victim, momentarily at
least, of an inimical environment. Scientific
curiosity, on the other hand, confesses no

such inadequacy. Even if this were all, it were not so bad; for the dignity of man still remains—"When he calls upon himself, he finds himself at home." And this distinction invests with something of its qualities all else that is. Man in trouble is so superior to his troubles that as the traveler ignores the dust of the road, so man looks quietly upon the host of besetting evils, sees them for what they are, and feels that it is enough to know that all their values, whether positive or negative, borrow something from his own creative self. Why, then, should he not take them one by one, as they come, and find each event self-justifying? This is the essence of independence. Who has it not is yet a slave puling for salvation. Who has it, though all else fail, himself fails not; for finding time continually to deal him strangely, he has but to say, "By Jove, this is strange; I shall find a special pleasure in this chronic disappointment."

So far the discussion has had in mind irremediable evils that one suffers in his own person. Unquestionably the scientific attitude shows at its best in dealing with such examples. On the other hand, an attitude that fits well in the case of one's own troubles may seem to betoken a lack of sympathy when applied to those of another. If such an attitude is incompatible with fellow-feeling, then it is imperative that some way be found to harmonize them. The harmony is certainly achieved in the person of many a wise and humane physician, to mention only one source of hope in our day. A sympathy that abandons itself to wallow in the woes of another is of questionable moral worth when judged by any but the sentimental. If public opinion says otherwise, public opinion must be reconciled by education to a more adequate exploitation of the scientific resources already under human control. On the other side, "to peep and botanize" upon a mother's grave need not involve desecration. Were it not for precisely the temper of mind that Wordsworth meant those words to belittle, mothers' graves would still be multiplying as prematurely as in the churchyards of his day. Knowledge must be mellowed by sympathy, but sympathy must in its turn be lighted by insight. After all, sentimentalism rather than science is the chief foe of any effective social bond. To take an extreme case in which detachment ran to humor, it is doubtful whether even the faithful in their heart of hearts thought sacrilegious the headline announcement of the passing of their leader, "Mary Baker Eddy stole home on an error."

Coming at the contrast of these two attitudes from another angle, we may say that resignation emphasizes the virtue of possession. And so strongly has the Western world entwined its values with possession as against creation that whatever experiences are not themselves possessive in nature are held to require justification through a far-off connection with possession. But this ideal need not always so mightily prevail. It is said that during the Japanese festival in honor of Ebisu, the God of honest hard work, as well as of wealth, the head man of the village calls out in a loud voice, as the procession approaches the shrine: "According to our annual custom, let us all laugh." There is a joy in creation and in activity as well as in possession. And this potential joy can with profit be made actual in fortifying us against the evils of life. If the nature of our candle is to burn at both ends, then why not find joy in the lovely light that it gives, even though it will not last through the night! This is a way of taking life that all men have had and most have lost; for it is essentially the attitude of childhood. The years bring as their inevitable yoke, the habit of evaluating everything in the light of something else coming on.

Nevertheless, this habit which urgent control necessitates may well be unlearned at the farthest frontier of control. The scientific way of life passes easily into the aesthetic way of life when the scientist no longer needs to control his material, and so it may for the common man when he no longer can control his fate. "A frank and somewhat headlong carriage," says Robert Louis Stevenson, "not looking too anxiously before, not dallying in maudlin regret over the past, stamps the man who is well armoured for this world." In the face of disease that is as yet incurable, of suffering that defies assuagement, of inevitable death, the stricken mind that is matured may yet carry on and still leave open the door to a growing mastery of what is now beyond our control. Resignation, like indiscriminate charity, is such a remedy as perpetuates—yea, spreads—the disease it alleviates. Scientific curiosity, on the other hand, touched with a sense of beauty, watches the on-going process, whether in oneself or in another, so intently as to discover any developing cues for control, but so intently indeed as to find the stream self-justifying should no such cues appear. Whether the philosophic mind sees life, with Walter Lippmann, "as comedy or high tragedy or plain farce, he would affirm that it is what it is, and that the wise man can enjoy it." What is true of life may, with Kipling's Tramp-Royal, be also affirmed of death—

What do it matter where or 'ow we die,
So long as we've our 'ealth to watch it all?

V

Predisposed in the beginning toward the scientific way of life as the nucleus of my own philosophy, I have now emerged at the end with something borrowed, something declined, from all the proffered guides. It is obvious how much I have accepted from William James in putting scientific curiosity at the center of my own attitude toward life. It was he who most emphatically taught me the cardinal virtues of tolerance and open-mindedness. It was he who showed me how to take my poignant desire for growth as a basic asset and then through respect for science to expand it into a philosophy. I deserted him as guide only when he seemed untrue to himself. He taught me to extend my curiosity to emotional and even occult material, though he did not reconcile me to the use of religious terms as finally descriptive of it. I prefer, despite his example, to call things by plain names when I see them clearly rather than by names that exploit the very curiosity whose edge they dull. He has, however, made me tolerant of those who count religious categories as final; for his experience as well as his teaching has helped me to glimpse the violence of storms that may terrorize into semi-submission the soul that dreamed of emancipation.

John Dewey has shown me that I am a part of an environment that far outreaches me, for the fringe of which I am the conscious focus; and he has made me realize that life cannot be lived wisely save in appreciative recognition of its debt to and duty toward society. I mature only through ac-

cepting responsibility; my responsibility
arises from liability; and liability is my community's grievous but fruitful way of calling
my attention to important consequences of
my action which otherwise I should never
see. His social way of life has convinced me
that these moral and creative forces are, in
varying degrees, resident in every man and
that, in whatever degree, they are so important that no oversight through social inertia
or class prejudice should be allowed to stand
in the way of complete exploitation of them
by and for the whole human community. I
have deserted him as guide only when he
seemed in his enthusiasm for community to
suggest that what things are for us mortals,
only this they are for and of themselves.
The values of community are too intimate
and final to need metaphysical illusion as
sanction. Experience in any sense meaningful to men is not final. It is a late comer-on,
and for aught that we know an early goer-
from, the cosmic scene. Dewey has taught
me to see it as final, however, for method
and for meaning; but man himself is by this
very fact revealed as episodic in an on-going
universe.

Josiah Royce has impressed me with the fact that this Deweyan society of which I am a functional part is itself a part of a still larger environment that average men cannot hope to control except by striking an attitude or through other equally magical means. Royce's "world of the powers" looms portentous over his optimistic foreground of postulates. His community that stands back of human communities loses conclusiveness for me as it acquires finality for him. His marvelous show of logic impresses me as it impressed both James and Santayana—"a screen for his heart . . . . a heart in which there was no clearness." Enthusiasm is not enough for a guide. Royce has, nevertheless, vitalized for me the notion and the experience of community; but he has left me alone with the human community in spite of all his ardor for the divine. He has, moreover, shown me the danger of losing the precious finite by straining after the elusive infinite. No one can read Royce without seeing that in philosophy the principle of audacity is perhaps at least as influential as the principle of parcimony. Since not a little of public opinion is determined by sound and fury,

Royce makes it easy for one to believe that from the point of view of social engineering it is necessary to have somebody affirm the principle of democracy as vociferously as Mussolini affirms the opposite, and to have somebody affirm the principle of pluralism as prolixly and as genially as Royce affirms the principle of a feudalistic monism. While I see every reason for supposing the nature of reality to be starker than Royce conceives it, he has taught me to see how small is the shadow cast by both man and men.

George Santayana has reinforced the scientific way of life by demonstrating how pitiable is the idealistic dependence upon logic when the order of events is material. What dialectic cannot do by magic, common sense may do when it becomes precise and potent as science. He has confirmed all my experience as to the irrelevance of wishful thinking and all my belief in science as the only basal way to improve the human lot. When, however, I have reached the boundary of control as regards both men and nature, the aesthetic way of life has taught me that religion is not the only recourse of impotence. Santayana talks much of religion, but always paradoxically: he believes, as the wag not unjustly characterized him, that there is no God and that Mary is his mother. But whatever one calls the fruits of spirit, Santayana has taught me to prize its career and gratefully to appropriate its significance for life.

The glory of man is, after all, in his peculiar faculty of uniting the past and the future in an expanded present. The waste of the evolutionary process often noted on lower levels, would be prodigious on the level of imagination if all ideas that are not programs of activity were discounted as mere lotus-lusting. Santayana has shown me the poverty of a too rigorous pragmatism in the definition of intelligence; and in doing so has crowned robust science with the artistic excesses of fancy. In showing me the significance and finality of the novel at each successive level of emergence, he has made available an acceptance of the universe more active than resignation, more passive than rebellion—the harvest of a quiet eye content merely to observe the passing show.

At the threshold of the realm of essence I have awaited his return from what I sus-

pected his one excursion into superstition—
his belief that essences antedate experience
and skirt it only accidentally. Not long,
however, did I have to wait; and when he re-
turned he taught me how fittingly essences
complete experience. Nor has he merely
shown me the significance of beauty; he has
also tutored me in the uncanny utility of wit.

That I grow sick and curse my being's source
If haply one day passes lacking mirth.

This way of life has taught me, indeed, that
he who has grace to see himself in true relation to others and to the world may often
smile at his fancies, laugh at his own infla-
tions, scoff at his own prejudices. On the
verge of being conquered by the world, man
masters fate in dying nobly. "By becoming
the spectator and confessor of his own death
and of universal mutation, he will," says
Santayana, "have identified himself with
what is spiritual in all spirits and masterful
in all apprehension." This is the victory that
overcometh the world, even understanding
and self-control.

What all these philosophers have taught
me, though with differential grace and wit, is

that there is no conclusion to philosophy until all life is concluded. Only pompous men seek to impose a philosophy; only wiseacres lay claim to all wisdom. Knowledge is power; and he who is presumptuous in claiming knowledge is not to be trusted with power. No man is good enough not to misuse unconditional power; and claims of authoritative wisdom can be counted upon in a world of limited economic goods sooner or later to show themselves at the stock exchange. Since not even philosophy can insure a good life without a modicum of the goods of life, the judicious man, and particularly in our day the wise woman, will watch those who offer to provide guaranteed beliefs—whether as religion or as philosophy—as he or she watches those who would sell authentic gold bricks.

So have I learned from our guides and from older guides of these guides. As earnest of this lesson I have in the summary shed the last vestige of authority—the editorial "we"—to speak only for myself. I now renounce even the prestige of print and lapse again into silence. The reader is at last alone, pondering, if it be so, the major moral of the best wise men—the moral that in the conduct of life there is no guide like oneself.

APPENDIX

For further guidance and delight the following selected books of these four philosophers are suggested, in the order listed:

ROYCE:

The Philosophy of Loyalty (1908)
The Religious Aspect of Philosophy (1885)
The Spirit of Modern Philosophy (1892)
The Conception of God (1897)
The Problem of Christianity (2 volumes) (1903)
The World and the Individual (2 volumes) (1900–1901)

JAMES:

Pragmatism (1907)
The Will to Believe, and Other Essays (1897)
Human Immortality (1898)
Psychology, Briefer Course (1892)
A Pluralistic Universe (1909)
Varieties of Religious Experience (1902)
Essays in Radical Empiricism (1912)

DEWEY:

School and Society (1899)
Influence of Darwin on Philosophy, and Other Essays (1910)
Human Nature and Conduct (1922)
The Public and Its Problems (1927)
Experience and Nature (1925)
Essays in Experimental Logic (1916)

SANTAYANA:

Winds of Doctrine (1913)
Dialogues in Limbo (1925)
Platonism and the Spiritual Life (1927)
Skepticism and Animal Faith (1923)
The Realm of Essence (1927)
The Life of Reason (5 volumes) (1905–6)

INDEX

PRINTED
IN U·S·A·